# The Angevin Empire

# The Angevin Empire

## Second Edition

JOHN GILLINGHAM
*Emeritus Professor of History, London School of Economics
and Political Science*

A member of the Hodder Headline Group
LONDON
Co-published in the United States of America by
Oxford University Press Inc., New York

First published in Great Britain in 2001 by
Arnold, a member of the Hodder Headline Group,
338 Euston Road, London NW1 3BH

http://www.arnoldpublishers.com

Co-published in the United States of America by
Oxford University Press Inc.,
198 Madison Avenue, New York, NY10016

The advice and information in this book are believed to be true and
accurate at the date of going to press, but neither the author nor the publisher
can accept any legal responsibility for any errors or omissions.

*British Library Cataloguing in Publication Data*
A catalogue record for this book is available from the British Library

*Library of Congress Cataloging-in-Publication Data*
A catalog record for this book is available from the Library of Congress

ISBN 0 340 74114 7 (hb)
ISBN 0 340 74115 5 (pb)

1 2 3 4 5 6 7 8 9 10

Production Editor: James Rabson
Production Controller: Martin Kerans
Cover Design: Terry Griffiths

Typeset in 11 on 13 pt Sabon by Cambrian Typesetters, Frimley, Surrey
Printed and bound in Great Britain by MPG Books Ltd, Bodmin, Cornwall

What do you think about this book? Or any other Arnold title?
Please send your comments to feedback.arnold@hodder.co.uk

*In memory of Tom Keefe*

# Contents

# List of maps

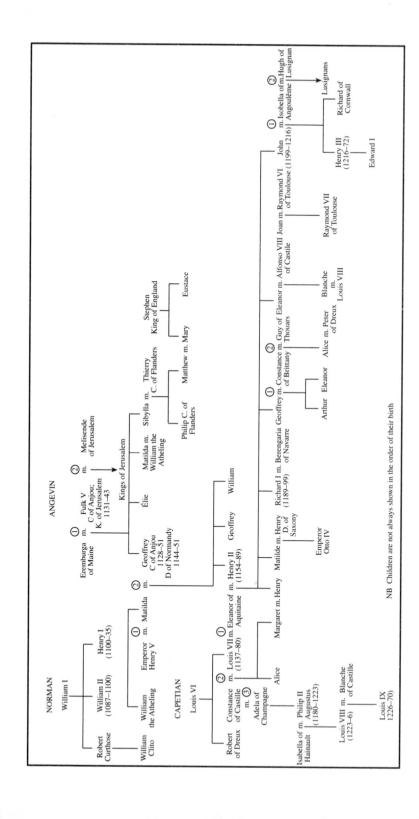

NORMAN

William I

Robert Curthose — William II (1087–1100) — Henry I (1100–35)

William Clito

William the Atheling — Emperor Henry V m. ① Matilda ② m.

CAPETIAN

Louis VI

Robert of Dreux — Louis VII m. ① Eleanor of Aquitaine m. ① Louis VII (1137–80) ② m. Constance of Castile m. ③ Adela of Champagne

Alice

Isabella of Hainault m. Philip II Augustus (1180–1223)

Louis VIII (1223–6) m. Blanche of Castille

Louis IX 1226–70

ANGEVIN

Eremburga of Maine m. ① Fulk V C of Anjou; K. of Jerusalem 1131–43 ② m. Melisende of Jerusalem

Geoffrey C of Anjou 1128–51 D of Normandy 1144–51

Élie

Kings of Jerusalem

Sibylla m. Thierry C. of Flanders

Matilda m. William the Atheling

Philip C. of Flanders

Matthew m. Mary

Stephen King of England

Eustace

Geoffrey C of Anjou 1128–51 D of Normandy 1144–51 m. ② Henry II (1154–89)

William

Geoffrey

Margaret m. Henry — Matilde m. Henry D. of Saxony — Richard I m. Berengaria (1189–99) of Navarre — Geoffrey m. Constance of Brittany — John (1199–1216) m. ① Isabella of m. Hugh of Angoulême Lusignan ②

Emperor Otto IV

Arthur Eleanor

Guy of Thouars m. ② Constance of Brittany

Alice m. Peter of Dreux

Alice m. Peter of Dreux

Eleanor m. Alfonso VIII of Castile

Blanche m. Louis VIII

Joan m. Raymond VI of Toulouse

Lusignans

Richard of Cornwall

Henry III (1216–72)

Raymond VII of Toulouse

Edward I

NB Children are not always shown in the order of their birth

# Preface to the Second Edition

This is a revised and expanded edition of a book first published in 1984 in the Edward Arnold series 'Foundations of Medieval History' (General editor, Michael Clanchy). The purpose of that series was to 'provide concise and authoritative introductions' which would 'enable students both to master the basic facts about a topic and to form their own point of view'. I hope that this second edition, although in all about 25 per cent longer than the first edition, does at least remain concise. In one respect, indeed, it is shorter. The words 'feudal' and 'vassal' appear slightly less often than in the first edition. This new edition is in part a result of the anniversary factor –1999 being the 800th anniversary of the death of Richard I and accession of King John. Three conferences, one on King John at Norwich, two on Richard I at Caen and Thouars, acted as a considerable stimulus to further reflection.

During the intervening years I have owed much to the congenial atmosphere at the meetings of the Battle Conference founded by R. Allen Brown, and to its proceedings, published annually as *Anglo-Norman Studies* – recently described by Frank Barlow as 'a golden treasury'. Battle's American equivalent, the Haskins Society, has performed a similarly valuable role; its newsletter, 'The Anglo-Norman Anonymous', published three times a year, being a useful and often entertaining way of keeping abreast of work in progress.

Since 1984 the study of royal government in England – a traditional strength of English historical writing – has gone on apace, but it is a particular pleasure here to note how much work is now being done on the French side of Plantagenet history by younger English scholars, several of them thanks to the encouragement and support given by Sir James Holt. I have in mind Judith Everard, Vincent Moss, Daniel Power, Kathleen Thompson and Nicholas Vincent. In this revision I have owed much to their scholarship. I have also had a great deal of help from Jane Martindale, and have benefited from Alban Gautier's kindness in supplying me with a copy of his unpublished *mémoire de maîtrise*: 'L'empire angevin: une invention des historiens?' No doubt about it.

There is a certain nostalgic pleasure in being able to hold Christopher Wheeler, Director of Humanities Publishing at Arnold, responsible for this new edition, since it was he who, nearly twenty years ago now, commissioned its first edition. I am grateful to him for never quite giving up on the attempt to persuade me to produce an expanded version. My thanks also to all those who have helped to see this book through the press: Susan Dunsmore, Emma Heyworth-Dunn and James Rabson.

September 2000

# 1 Introduction

By the Angevin Empire I mean the assemblage of lands held by the family of the counts of Anjou (the Angevins) in the 80 or so years after 1144. In 1144 the count of Anjou, Geoffrey Plantagenet, became duke of Normandy; in 1152 his successor, Henry, acquired Aquitaine (by virtue of his marriage to Eleanor of Aquitaine); in 1154 Henry also became king of England. He was, in the words of several contemporaries, 'in extent of his dominions a greater king than any of his predecessors'. For the next 50 years, within more or less stable boundaries, this vast accumulation of territories, stretching from the Scottish border to the Pyrenees, was ruled by a series of princes who could claim to be the most powerful rulers in Western Europe: Henry II, Richard I, John. Then in 1202–4 John lost Anjou, Normandy and much of Poitou (the northern part of the duchy of Aquitaine) to Philip Augustus, the most successful of the Capetian kings of France; in the 1220s the Capetians completed their conquest of Poitou. Thereafter, although the Plantagenets continued to rule both England and Gascony, as well as some other territories – Wales, Ireland and the Channel Islands – the structure of their lands was very different from what it had been in the second half of the twelfth century. Then the political centre of gravity had been in France; the Angevins were French princes who numbered England amongst their possessions. But from the 1220s onwards the centre of gravity was clearly in England; the Plantagenets had become kings of England who occasionally visited Gascony. The Angevin decades, though they stand squarely within a very much longer period (say, from the eleventh to the fifteenth centuries) during which 'English' and 'French' history were inextricably interwoven, do, none the less, possess a distinct character of their own. The 'great transformation'[1] of the early thirteenth century makes of the Angevin Empire a political entity with a history which is structurally different not only from that of the preceding Norman Empire but different also from subsequent Plantagenet history.

1 J. Le Patourel, 'The Plantagenet dominions', *History*, 50 (1965), p. 2.

## THE EMPIRE WITH NO NAME

Although for some 50 years (1154–1204) the Angevin Empire was the dominant polity in Western Europe, there was, so far as we know, no contemporary name for this assemblage of territories. When anyone wanted to refer to them there were only clumsy circumlocutions available – for example, the 'our kingdom and everything subject to our rule wherever it may be' used by Henry II, or one of his chancery clerks, in a letter to Frederick Barbarossa in 1157. Nearly 50 years later the continuator of the Annals of St-Aubin (Angers) referred to the lands to which John had succeeded as 'the whole of the kingdom which had belonged to his father'. There was no equivalent to the term *regnum Norman-Anglorum* devised by the Norman author of the Hyde chronicle to describe Henry I's Anglo-Norman realm. But this chronicler was writing more than 50 years after the Norman Conquest. Fifty years after the Angevin conquest of England, most of the continental lands of the Plantagenets had been lost and, with them, the need to invent a new label had gone.

The term 'Angevin Empire' is a product of the nineteenth century, coined by Kate Norgate[2] in 1887. Her coinage signalled a significant shift away from the assumption that what really counted during the reigns of the kings of England from Henry II to John were purely English matters: the Becket dispute, the making of the Common Law, Magna Carta. This was the assumption that had dominated historical writing since the seventeenth century. For English authors, such as Macaulay, the French possessions were an encumbrance which endangered the sound development of a genuinely English polity.

> Had the Plantagenets, as at one time seemed likely, succeeded in uniting all France under their government, it is probable that England would never have had an independent existence. The revenues of her great proprietors would have been spent in festivities and diversions on the banks of the Seine. The noble language of Milton and Burke would have remained a rustic dialect, contemptuously abandoned to the use of boors. England owes her escape from such calamities to an event which her historians have generally represented as disastrous.[3]

It was, as Stubbs put it, following Macaulay's train of thought, 'the fortunate incapacity of John' that enabled England 'to cut herself

---

2 K. Norgate, *England under the Angevin Kings*, 2 vols (London, 1887), vol. 2, p. 491.
3 T. B. Macaulay, *History of England* (London, 1849) in 1907 reprint, ed. T. F. Henderson, p. 4.

free from Normandy'.[4] On the other hand, for French historians such as Michelet, Henry and his sons ruled an 'English empire' – a term sometimes found in French guidebooks even today. They were Englishmen who had to be driven out of France. Against this historiographical background Norgate's insight was to be an immensely fruitful one.

Since then her choice of the term 'Angevin' has, on the whole, caused little difficulty for historians. Some have preferred 'Plantagenet'. But although Henry II's father Count Geoffrey was known as Plantagenet, it was not until the fifteenth century that this term came to be used as a family name, and for the story that the name came from a sprig of broom (*Planta genista*) that he liked to wear in his hat to be put into writing we have to wait until the nineteenth century. It can be argued that one anachronistic term is as good as another, but since Plantagenet as a dynastic label was a term coined at a time when kings of England claimed that France was theirs by right of inheritance, I have a slight preference for a term which lacks this particular political connotation. In twelfth-century usage 'angevin' was the continental equivalent of the insular term 'sterling'. In 1184 when Henry II levied a tax in aid of the Holy Land, his subjects in England were assessed in sterling; his subjects 'in the land of the king of England on this side of the sea' (for Henry was then in France) in angevins. None the less there were political implications here too. When Philip Augustus conquered Normandy the angevin penny became a prohibited coin.

In the last hundred years the term 'empire' has been much more controversial. Unquestionably if used in conjunction with atlases in which Henry II's lands are coloured red, it is a dangerous term, for then overtones of the British Empire are unavoidable and politically crass. But in ordinary English usage 'empire' can mean nothing more specific than an extensive territory, especially an aggregate of many states, ruled over by a single ruler. When coupled with 'Angevin', it should, if anything, imply a French rather than a 'British' empire. Moreover, the word 'empire' does at least have some slight support in contemporary usage – which is more than can be said for alternatives such as Angevin or Plantagenet 'dominions' or 'commonwealth'. Contemporary authors sometimes used the Latin word *imperium*. Indeed one early thirteenth-century English author made the bold claim that the king of England ruled over not a *regnum* (kingdom),

---

4 W. Stubbs, *The Constitutional History of England*, 4th edn (Oxford, 1883) vol. 1, p. 482.

but an *imperium*. He had in mind English power within Britain. Other writers used the word *imperium* in its more general meaning of 'rule' as when Richard FitzNigel, the author of *The Dialogue of the Exchequer,* speaking of Henry II, wrote *suum dilataverit imperium,* 'he extended his rule'. Richard may well have had the French word 'empire' in his mind, but this too has a wider range of meanings than the English word 'empire'. The Old French *Song of Dermot and the Earl* contains a scene in which King Dermot of Leinster, speaking to Henry II, referred to 'les baruns de tun empire'. This may mean 'the barons of your empire', but it could also be rendered as 'the barons of your command', i.e 'of your army'. The fact is that Henry II – despite being FitzEmpress – was never called 'Emperor' even though contemporary Capetian and Castilian kings were occasionally accorded this title. Nor, despite the possibility that Richard I was crowned with the heavy 'imperial crown' which his grandmother had brought back from Germany in 1125 did the Angevin ruler ever aspire to an imperial coronation.[5] There is no contemporary evidence to support the charge, brought many years later by Gerald de Barri, that Henry II's ambitions extended even *ad Romanum imperium.* The author of the early thirteenth-century *Histoire des ducs de Normandie* believed that Richard I turned down an offer of the German imperial throne in 1198, but in reality the king was content to promote the candidature of his nephews, Henry and Otto of Brunswick. The fact is that there never was an Angevin Emperor either holy or (in view of the Angevin legend of their descent from the devil) unholy. The Angevin Empire did not survive for long enough to become a traditional part of the European political scene; nor, during its term of existence, was it expected to survive. But it does not necessarily follow from this that it could not have done.

Those modern historians who have doubted the usefulness of the term 'Angevin Empire' have posed a series of questions. Did it possess a 'centralized administrative structure'? Was its ruler a genuine 'sovereign' or did he owe allegiance to other rulers? How was it thought of? As a unified territorial state? Or as a motley collection of lands with only their shared ruler holding them together in a precarious unity? Were the various dominions in the process of being welded together into a unity which would bear comparison with similar 'empires', with the union of Anjou, Touraine and Maine into a

5 K. Leyser, 'Frederick Barbarossa, Henry II and the hand of St James', *English Historical Review*, 90 (1975).

single 'Greater Anjou', for example – or did they differ too substantially in status, structure and culture for that ever to be possible? Their answers to these questions have led historians to conclude that the term 'Angevin Empire' is inappropriate. The notion of an Anglo-French or Anglo-Angevin state with a fairly long life span has been seen as an unrealistic reflection of an early twentieth-century Entente Cordiale. Thus, the clear conclusion of a conference held at Fontevraud in 1986 was that it was permissible to speak of 'espace Plantagenêt' but that was all. There was no Plantagenet state and no Plantagenet Empire. I propose to ignore this conclusion but not the questions that led to it. No matter what label we choose to adopt, the questions remain. They are not quite so easy to answer as is sometimes assumed.

The major difficulty confronting the historian of the Angevin Empire lies in the nature of his evidence. In two fundamental ways it is badly skewed: chronologically and geographically. In the first place there is immeasurably more evidence – including whole new *types* of evidence – after 1199 than before 1199. In these circumstances there is a danger of assuming that men were doing things after 1199 which they had not done before, when it may be that they *had* done these same things but either no record was kept or none has survived. In the second place there is immeasurably more evidence, both chronicle evidence and record evidence, for England than for any other part of the Angevin dominions. In these circumstances there is a danger of attributing to England an importance which it may not have possessed. In one way England undeniably *was* the most important part – it gave the ruler a royal crown. Since the first element in his title was then *Rex Anglorum* this meant that the most convenient shorthand way of referring to him was as king of England or even – Frenchman though he was – as the English king, *il reis Engles*. But it does not follow from this that England was the most important part in other ways as well.

Once stated, the dangers are obvious. What is not quite so obvious is how they are to be coped with. That too will soon become obvious to the reader. But the main problem with this book is that it attempts to fill a much needed gap. Everyone knows that the emergence of the national kingdoms of England and France was inevitable. The very idea of an effective political structure cutting across those predestined frontiers is absurd.

# 2 The making of the Angevin Empire

## FRANCE AND ENGLAND IN 1150

A political map of north-western Europe in 1150 would make clear the pre-eminence of the king of France. Louis VII (1137–80) ruled not only the traditional lands of his family, the Capetian royal principality which stretched from Compiègne in the north to the neighbourhood of Bourges in the south; by virtue of his marriage to Eleanor, he was also duke of Aquitaine, lord of a territory which covered roughly one third of the area of modern France. There were, of course, other powerful princes in this region: Stephen, king of England, Geoffrey Plantagenet, duke of Normandy and count of Anjou, Theobald, count of Blois and Champagne. But none of them was quite in Louis's league. Moreover by 1154 Stephen, Geoffrey and Theobald were all dead and, given what we know about their plans for the future of their lands, it is well within the bounds of possibility that they would have been succeeded by five different men: Eustace, son of Stephen, in England; Henry and Geoffrey, sons of Geoffrey, in Normandy and Anjou; Theobald and Henry, sons of Theobald, in Blois and Champagne. By 1154, in other words, the pre-eminence of the king of France might have been even more marked.

This, of course, is not what happened. Instead Geoffrey's son Henry not only kept both Normandy and Anjou, he also, by one means or other, seized control of both England and Aquitaine. By 1154 from being just once prince among many others, he had become the most powerful ruler in Europe, richer even than the Emperor. Moreover, he now completely overshadowed his own nominal overlord, the king of France. How had this sudden transformation come about? Was it the result of genealogical accident? Or of a series of political opportunities unscrupulously exploited? Or the final working out of some long-term plan? Was it chance or design which lay behind the creation of the Angevin Empire and if the latter, then whose design?

Many historians have suggested that the idea of an empire comprising both the lands of Anjou and the Anglo-Norman state was first conceived in the astute political brain of King Henry I of England (1100–35; duke of Normandy from 1106). Undeniably it was Henry who in 1127 initiated the negotiations which led to the crucial marriage between the heir to Anjou and the heiress to England and Normandy. But it can be argued that the original architect of the Angevin Empire was not so much Henry as the man he was negotiating with: Fulk V, count of Anjou. It was, after all, the dynasty of the counts of Anjou which turned out to be the chief beneficiary of that marriage alliance.

## THE COUNTS OF ANJOU

Throughout the tenth and eleventh centuries the counts of Anjou belonged to a group of princes who were alternately enemies and allies in the struggle for land and power in northern and western Gaul. Among their rivals were the rulers of Normandy and Brittany, the counts of Poitou, Blois, Nantes and Maine, even indeed the kings of France – for although the Capetians held a grander title, in terms of land and power, they were at this stage just one of the princes. By the end of the eleventh century the Angevin counts had a well-developed sense of dynastic self-consciousness. In a remarkable chronicle of which only a fragment still survives, Count Fulk IV of Anjou set down the achievement of his ancestors. In essence it is a catalogue of castles built, sieges laid and battles fought, a description of the ways by which military means – the spade and the sword – could be used to obtain political ends. By 1096 Fulk IV claimed to be ruler of Touraine, Maine and Nantes as well as of Anjou but in Maine and in Nantes men may well have told a different story. The undeniable success of the counts of Anjou lay in their gradual acquisition of the Touraine, inch by inch, castle by castle, at the expense of their eastern neighbours, the counts of Blois. The possession of Tours, the city of St Martin, *Martinopolis,* an important market and a vital communications centre, gave the Angevins a tremendous strategic advantage; the building of the great castles of Chinon, Loches and Loudun showed that they were determined to hold on to it.

But castles and campaigns were not the only tools of politics. As society became more settled and prosperous, so inheritance customs developed to allow – in the absence of sons – daughters to succeed to principalities as well as to landed estates. The twelfth century is a century of heiresses. To an ambitious politician capturing heiresses came to be at least as important as capturing castles.[1] For years, for example, Fulk IV was determined to obtain the hand of Eremburga, heiress of Hélie, count of Maine. Eventually he succeeded in marrying her to his own son and heir, Fulk V (1109–28). Hélie's death, in 1110, was followed by the union of Anjou and Maine. The acquisition of Touraine and Maine were considerable achievements and if Fulk V had looked about him at the beginning of the year 1127 he would have had little cause to feel dissatisfied. The Angevin dynasty had done well. On the other hand, the main rivals of the Angevins had done even better. The dukes of Normandy had conquered England; the counts of Poitou (who were also dukes of Aquitaine) had obtained Gascony; and only recently, in 1125, the count of Blois had inherited Champagne. In the course of the next eighteen months the prospects of the counts of Anjou changed dramatically. By the summer of 1128 Fulk himself was designated heir to one kingdom, while his elder son Geoffrey was heir to another. For the Angevins 1128 was an *annus mirabilis*.

## 1128: THE MARRIAGE OF GEOFFREY AND MATILDA

It all began with a seemingly unrelated event, the murder of Count Charles of Flanders on 2 March 1127 as he knelt at morning prayer in the church of St Donatien in Bruges. Charles had no children so the turmoil which followed his murder was exacerbated by a struggle over the succession to the county. By early April one of the candidates, William Clito, son of Robert Curthose, duke of Normandy, had obtained a clear advantage over his rivals. For Henry I this was alarming news. Over the last 15 years it was precisely his nephew Clito who had been the main threat to his secure hold on the Anglo-Norman realm. If Clito, who already enjoyed the support of Louis VI of France, were able to employ the great wealth of Flanders in pursuit of his claim to England and Normandy, the outlook for his uncle was black indeed. Naturally Henry I did his best to queer Clito's pitch in Flanders, but at the same time he looked around for allies of his own – and the most

1 According to one twelfth-century historian, Ralph of Diceto, Anjou extended its dominion over neighbouring peoples not by slaughtering them but by marrying them: 'Et tu felix Andegavia nube.'

obvious direction in which to look was towards Anjou. Nine years earlier a coalition of France, Flanders and Anjou, in support of William Clito, had nearly unseated Henry. It was in order to break up this hostile coalition that Henry had gone to the lengths of arranging the marriage of his only legitimate son, William (later drowned in the White Ship disaster, 1120), to Fulk V's daughter Matilda. So, in 1127, in order to prevent a renewal of the France–Flanders–Anjou alliance, Henry approached Count Fulk with a new proposal. His daughter Matilda should marry Fulk's son and heir, Geoffrey Plantagenet, later known as *le Bel*.

By this date Matilda was a widow. In 1110 she had been married to the Emperor Henry V and she was still in Germany when her brother, William, was drowned. Henry I's immediate reaction to the death of his son had been to marry again. According to William of Malmesbury, in Henry I's view the point of sex was politics not pleasure, yet despite this determined attitude – or perhaps because of it – he and his new queen, Alice of Louvain, were unable to produce an heir to the throne. As the years passed, the problem of the succession loomed ever larger. Then, after the death of the Emperor Henry V in 1125, it occurred to Henry that it might be possible to arrange for Matilda to succeed. Clearly it would not be easy for in 1125 there was still only a single precedent for female succession to a throne: the case of Urraca in the kingdom of Castile-Leon in 1109 – and given the turbulence of Urraca's reign (1109–26) this was hardly an encouraging precedent. Henry I's powers of persuasion were, however, formidable. In January 1127 the Anglo-Norman barons and prelates swore an oath to accept Matilda as ruler after her father's death. From then on whoever married her could expect in due course to become *iure uxoris* king of England and duke of Normandy. Just a few months later the unforeseeable crisis triggered off by the murder of the count of Flanders meant that this man was Geoffrey of Anjou.

Naturally it took time to work out all the details, but by the summer of 1128 everything was arranged. On Whitsunday 10 June 1128 Henry I knighted Geoffrey at Rouen, a magnificent ceremony which culminated in the new 14-year-old knight being girded with a sword reputedly forged by Wayland the Smith. Then Henry, Geoffrey and Matilda rode to meet Geoffrey's father in Le Mans and there, in a city which had long been a bone of contention between dukes of Normandy and counts of Anjou, the wedding which brought about the union of the two families were celebrated on 17

June – and for the next three weeks. Then, while Henry returned to Normandy, Fulk V of Anjou, his son and his daughter-in-law continued the celebrations. The tumultuous reception they received from the clergy and people of Angers left no room to doubt that, so far as the court of Anjou was concerned, Count Fulk had scored a diplomatic triumph: the first great step in the making of the Angevin Empire.

For the son of a count to marry the daughter of a king and the widow of an empress was no bad match – from an Angevin point of view. But how did it look to the Normans? For that 14-year-old boy to be offered, in addition, the prospect of succeeding to the throne of a great power was a very fine thing indeed – so fine indeed that, in their study of the subject, Hollister and Keefe doubted whether Henry can really have intended to make Geoffrey his successor.[2] They argued that Geoffrey's role was to provide his wife with sons, uphold her interests and, for his own part, to be content with Anjou. His job was to act, as Orderic Vitalis put it, as 'his wife's hired soldier'. But Orderic's words were written not in 1127–28 but in 1141, at a time when Geoffrey very clearly had not succeeded to the throne. Orderic, like almost every other chronicler of these events, knew what had actually happened after Henry I's death in 1135 and he wrote with all the advantages and disadvantages of hindsight. The one chronicler whose account does seem to have been written *before* 1135, indeed before 1130, is the author, probably Symeon of Durham, of a *History of the Kings* and he notes that at the time of the betrothal it was agreed that if Henry I died without a legitimate son then his son-in-law would succeed. This explicit contemporary statement can be supported by an argument from probability. Given the threat which Clito posed throughout the whole negotiating period from March 1127 to June 1128 it is hard to see how Henry could have offered anything less. By the summer of 1128 even Henry's father-in-law, the duke of Louvain, was prepared to fight on Clito's behalf. Henry was in no position to dictate terms. Fulk of Anjou's negotiating position, on the other hand, was becoming relatively stronger. Early in 1128 ambassadors from the Holy Land arrived in France. They came to announce that Melisende, daughter of King Baldwin II of Jerusalem, had been formally recognized as heiress and that whomever she married would become king when

---

2   C. W. Hollister and T. K. Keefe, 'The making of the Angevin Empire', *Journal of British Studies*, 12 (1973).

her father died. Attracted by this inducement, Fulk negotiated his own betrothal to Melisende. On 31 May 1128, less than three weeks before his son's wedding, Fulk took the cross. In other words the marriage of Geoffrey and Matilda was a marriage between a king's daughter and a man who would soon be able to describe himself (as we know he did) as a king's son. Fulk's prestige was visibly rising while Henry I's position continued to remain precarious. All in all there seems no good reason to doubt that in 1127–8 Fulk V negotiated his son's take-over of the Anglo-Norman realm in circumstances strikingly similar to those in which he himself had earlier taken over Maine and was now about to take over the kingdom of Jerusalem.

Whether or not Anjou and the Anglo-Norman state would remain united for long was, of course, another question. Much would depend on biological accident, on the number of children, in particular sons, born to Geoffrey and Matilda. Unquestionably Henry I and Fulk must have wondered what the future had in store. Above all Henry must have given some thought to the possibility that there would be no children. After all, there were no children of Matilda's first marriage. Was his daughter barren? If she was barren, would the Anglo-Norman realm then pass into the hands of her husband's family? Were William the Conqueror's descendants to be deprived of the realm of their great ancestor? It is not hard to guess what Henry I's reaction to this possibility would have been; nor, though there is no direct evidence, is it difficult to see what he could try to do about it. In Jerusalem Baldwin II was faced with the same prospect and we know what he did. In 1131 he decided that he should be succeeded by three persons jointly: Fulk, Melisende and their 2-year-old son. Similarly Henry I could have tied the succession jointly to Geoffrey, Matilda and their children, not granted it to Geoffrey to do with as he liked. If there were no children by this arrangement the realm would revert to another kinsman of Henry I's, perhaps to one of his nephews, Theobald or Stephen of Blois, not to a kinsman of Geoffrey's. On the other hand, if there were children they would succeed. In other words, if Geoffrey survived Matilda and married again, he was not to try to push aside Matilda's children to make room for the offspring of his second wife. There was indeed an episode of this kind in the recent history of the Angevin family. Fulk V himself was an example of a younger half-brother who received preferential treatment. All this explains why Henry I is reported as having been delighted by the birth of his grandson (in 1133) and why that boy (later Henry II) was explicitly described as 'the heir to the

Kingdom'. The birth of a second grandson, Geoffrey, in 1134 made it quite probable that Anjou and the Anglo-Norman realm would in time go their separate ways again: the maternal inheritance for Henry, the patrimony for Geoffrey.

## THE WAR OF NORMAN SUCCESSION

To negotiate a treaty was one thing; to implement its terms quite another. If Geoffrey and Matilda were to succeed to Henry's throne then they would need to prepare the ground during the old king's lifetime. They would need some kind of power base in England and Normandy, control of castles and a party of supporters. It is clear that they tried to obtain such a base and that they failed. They failed because had they succeeded there would have existed two centres of authority in the realm: theirs (as heirs presumptive) and the king's. This Henry was not prepared to allow. He refused to relinquish control over any castle in either England or Normandy and he confiscated the estates of those nobles whom he suspected of supporting Matilda and Geoffrey. By 1135 Henry I was quarrelling openly and violently with his designated heirs. This quarrel had the effect of re-opening old divisions within the Norman baronage. By driving those magnates who remained loyal to Henry into opposition to Geoffrey and Matilda this meant that when the old king died they would find it difficult to come to terms with his chosen successors. In this sense it was Henry himself who provoked the succession dispute which followed his death. Even at the end of his life he still wanted his daughter and son-in-law to succeed, but he had been unable to bring himself to take the measures which would have enabled them to do so. Henry I had been an outstandingly able and successful king, the master-politician of his age, but even he – like many other competent kings – failed to cope with the tensions of the succession question. It was for this reason that Henry of Huntingdon portrayed Henry as a king in a permanent state of anxiety. 'Each of his triumphs only made him worry lest he lose what he had gained; therefore though he seemed to be the most fortunate of kings, he was in truth the most miserable.'

Henry's ultimate failure made it inevitable that Geoffrey and Matilda would have to fight for their inheritance. And fight they did. Eventually, after no less than ten years of sustained campaigning, they were rewarded by a partial achievement of their ambition: the conquest of Normandy. Their attacks had not been mere raids, as is sometimes suggested, but serious attempts to conquer. The two chroniclers best placed to observe events, Orderic Vitalis and Robert of Torigni, both commented on the scale of Geoffrey's invasions and, in Orderic's case, on the ferocity of the fighting. If even this partial success had taken a long time, this is hardly surprising. Geoffrey and Matilda had faced an uphill struggle. The political structure of the Anglo-Norman realm meant that once Stephen of Blois had been recognized as king in England he was in a very strong position in Normandy as well. From then on the Norman barons could give their allegiance to someone else only at the risk of seeing their English estates taken away from them. There were a few nobles who took a different view but, by and large, those with most to lose felt that they had to support Stephen. Right from the start of their campaign to win their due inheritance, Geoffrey and Matilda found themselves opposed by the most powerful magnates of the Anglo-Norman state, men like Robert of Gloucester and the Beaumont brothers, Waleran of Meulan and Robert of Leicester.

If they had been able to prevent Stephen from carrying out his remarkable coup, then it might have been a different story, but this they were in no position to do. When, at the end of November 1135, the news came that Henry I was dying, they were in their own dominions, either in Anjou or Maine. Stephen, on the other hand, was in his county of Boulogne. This accident of geography gave Stephen a head start, an advantage which he exploited to the full in three hectic weeks after Henry's death. On 22 December he was crowned and anointed king at Westminster. But it was not only the Angevins who were put at a disadvantage by Stephen's relative proximity to London at the crucial moment. So too was Stephen's elder brother, Theobald count of Blois and Champagne. He was still discussing terms with a group of Norman barons who were prepared to offer the throne to him when the news came that Stephen was already crowned. These barons, including Robert of Gloucester, at once announced that they would now prefer to support Stephen 'on account of the honours which they held in both countries'.

With Theobald's reluctant withdrawal from the fray, the struggle for the Anglo-Norman succession came down to a straight fight between Stephen and the Angevins. Geoffrey had in fact acted with dispatch. As soon as he heard of King Henry's death he sent Matilda to Normandy to take possession of her right. Since she was the legitimate heiress it was reasonable to hope that she would create a better

— and therefore a more effective — impression if she came in peace rather than at the head of a foreign army. Her husband and their troops followed, some distance behind. By this means they rapidly gained possession of some important ducal fortresses including Domfront, Argentan and Exmes; in addition they were able to put two powerful marcher lords, William Talvas and Juhel de Mayenne, in possession of their seigneuries. This gave the Angevins a foothold in southern Normandy, one which they never relinquished. But hopes of further swift advance were dashed by news of a rebellion in their rear. Robert of Sablé, the most powerful baron in the north east of Anjou, chose to exploit this critical moment in the fortunes of the comital family to press claims of his own by force of arms. Geoffrey returned to Anjou. The impetus was lost and throughout the rest of Normandy men were free to ponder the implications of Stephen's success in England without having to worry about an Angevin army breathing down their necks.

Not until September 1136 was Geoffrey free to invade again. Conditions in Normandy, meanwhile, had been unsettled; several private wars had broken out. Stephen had not taken the opportunity to visit the duchy in the summer and restore order. Undoubtedly some of his supporters were disappointed by this delay and, in Stephen's failure to capitalize on his initial advantage, Count Geoffrey may well have seen some grounds for cautious optimism. None the less it was clear that he faced a daunting military task and he had accordingly mustered a very large army. In addition to the levies of Anjou and Maine he attracted some powerful allies to his banner, including the count of Vendôme and, most important of all, the duke of Aquitaine. In the face of this overwhelming strength, Stephen's commanders, Waleran of Meulan and Alan of Brittany, opted for discretion. As Geoffrey drove northwards as far as Lisieux, threatening to cut the duchy into two, they withdrew to a safe distance, first of all setting fire to Lisieux to prevent it from falling, undamaged, into Angevin hands. But Geoffrey retained the initiative and his position was further strengthened by Matilda's arrival at the head of yet more troops. In this crisis of his fortunes in Normandy, the absent king's cause was saved by two unexpected strokes of luck. First, Count Geoffrey was wounded in the foot and had to be taken back to Anjou in a litter. Second, an outbreak of diarrhoea brought about the disintegration of the Angevin army. In Orderic's words, the invaders had to run for home leaving a trail of filth behind them.

By the time Geoffrey and his followers had recovered sufficiently to make another attempt, Stephen had arrived in the duchy. In military terms the campaign of 1137 ended in a confused stalemate. On the other hand Stephen's Norman supporters were singularly unimpressed by what they saw of his accomplishments as a politician and their sense of disillusion can only have lightened Geoffrey's task. By the time of his next invasion, in June 1138, Geoffrey had persuaded no less a person than Robert of Gloucester to join him. This meant that he won several valuable ducal strongpoints, above all Caen and Bayeux, without having to fight for them. The defection of Robert of Gloucester must have been a bitter blow for Stephen. Despite this, the king's position remained relatively strong. Even Falaise, halfway between Caen and Argentan, still held out and in other parts of Normandy the Angevins could make little or no headway. It was increasingly clear that if they were going to overcome Stephen in Normandy then they would have to challenge his authority in England. Political morality as well as expediency made it essential that they carry the struggle to Stephen. Now that Robert of Gloucester had thrown in his lot with them they were obliged to help him save his vast English possessions from the king's anger. So, in 1139, Matilda and Robert crossed the Channel while Geoffrey stayed behind to maintain the pressure in Normandy and keep a watchful eye on his own volatile barons.

In the end this strategy worked. Normandy was won, not in Normandy, but in England. The capture of Stephen at the battle of Lincoln (2 February 1141) was immediately followed by the collapse of his position in Normandy as well as in England. By April 1141 Geoffrey was in control of almost the entire duchy west of the Seine and east of a line between Bayeux and Domfront. During the early summer of 1141, when the Angevins were on the verge of triumphant success both in England and Normandy, Stephen's only hope was that his ally, the king of France, conscious of the threat which the union of England, Normandy and Anjou might pose to his own kingdom, would intervene in the duchy and keep the Angevins at bay. Soon after Easter 1141, however, Louis VII set out, not for Rouen but in the opposite direction, towards Toulouse. In 1137 he had married Eleanor the heiress of Aquitaine and with that immense southern duchy at his disposal, the king of France saw little reason to be disturbed by changes in the political constellation of the north. In the end, Stephen was saved by his enemies as much as by his allies. The Empress Matilda's arrogance and inability to be magnanimous in victory meant that by September 1141 she had thrown away a won position. While Geoffrey held on to the gains he had made in Normandy, in England Matilda was driven back almost to square one. Presumably if she had secured the triumph which was within her grasp, Geoffrey, as well as becoming duke of Normandy, would have followed her across the Channel and would have been crowned king of England. But in the aftermath of the setback of autumn 1141 the hitherto united Angevin front was broken and a new family arrangement had to be worked out.

Matilda needed help in England; Geoffrey was much more interested in completing the conquest of Normandy. In 1142 he was begged to come to England and he refused. His attempt to soften the impact of this refusal by sending his 9-year-old eldest son in his place almost certainly involved his acquiescence in a re-definition of roles. Geoffrey had chosen to turn his back on England. Should it be conquered, then young Henry would be crowned, not jointly with his father, but alone. Geoffrey would have to be content to be duke of Normandy. But first Normandy had to be taken. In 1142 he overran the Avranchin and Stephen's own county of Mortain. In 1143 he completed the conquest of western Normandy (with the fall of Cherbourg) and launched his first attacks across the Seine. In 1144 Rouen surrendered and, with the traditional ducal capital in his hands, Geoffrey had himself formally invested as duke. In return for the cession of Gisors he obtained both recognition of his new title from Louis VII and military assistance in mopping up the remnants of resistance in eastern Normandy. His brother-in-law, Count Thierry of Flanders, also lent a hand, so when Arques, the last of Stephen's strongholds, fell in 1145, there could be no doubt that Duke Geoffrey was master of Normandy.

Despite this he made no effort to conquer England. His wife and her supporters were left to themselves to carry on a war which at times they seemed to be in danger of losing. Yet whatever setbacks they suffered Geoffrey remained on the Continent. Perhaps he simply preferred to live at a safe distance from his wife. But doubtless there were other reasons. Above all else Geoffrey was a count of Anjou and the defence and extension of his rights in and around Anjou itself were always his first priority. This had been the case during the Norman succession crisis of 1135–36 and was to be so again. From a strictly Angevin point of view, even the triumph in Normandy brought problems in its wake. Now that Geoffrey was lord of more than one principality it seemed to his younger brother Helie that there should be something to spare for him. He demanded Maine and, when this was refused, rebelled. This revolt had hardly been suppressed and Helie put in prison (where he died), than Geoffrey found himself engaged in yet another feud. His opponent was Gerald Berlay, lord of Montreuil-Bellay on the southern border of Anjou, in a region where the rights of the counts of Anjou and dukes of Aquitaine were intermingled. This quarrel and the consequent struggle for control of the castle of Montreuil-Bellay were to drag on for four years, become one of the most famous of all twelfth-century sieges and involve many of Geoffrey's neighbours, notably the king of France. Louis VII, indeed, had not only financed some of Gerald's activities, he had also appointed him seneschal of Poitou, and he was furious when Geoffrey captured and imprisoned Gerald.

It is in the context of his overriding concern for the problems of Anjou proper that we have to see Geoffrey's transfer of Normandy, early in 1150, to his eldest son. We should not, however, make too much of this transfer. Geoffrey had in fact associated Henry with him in the government of Normandy before 1150 and, though he dropped the title duke, he himself continued to play a dominant role in Norman affairs after this date. In essence the 'transfer' was an example of a custom now known as 'anticipatory association of the heir',[3] a fairly routine practice among eleventh- and early twelfth-century French nobles. A charter of 1145 implies that at that time Geoffrey had envisaged Henry succeeding to Anjou as well.[4] But as his second son Geoffrey grew older he may have changed his mind, perhaps encouraged to do so by Louis VII who would doubtless have preferred to see Anjou and Normandy in separate hands. Since it seems that in 1150 Henry was not given the title 'count of Anjou' in addition to that of 'duke of Normandy', it rather looks as though his father now had other plans for Anjou.

## THE CRISIS OF 1151–53

In 1150 the political situation was still very fluid. There could be no reasonable expectation that Henry Plantagenet was on the brink of creating an Angevin Empire markedly bigger than any of the other 'dynastic empires' characteristic of the eleventh and twelfth centuries. Indeed, his main rival, Stephen, had by no means given up

3 A. W. Lewis, 'Anticipatory association of the heir in early Capetian France', *American Historical Review*, 83 (1978).
4 M. Chibnall, *The Empress Matilda* (Oxford, 1991), 145.

hope of recovering Normandy. Now that Louis VII was at odds with the Angevins over their treatment of Gerald of Montreuil-Bellay an effective military alliance between the kings of England and France was very much on the cards. For this reason Geoffrey and his son were delighted when, in 1151, Louis decided to recognize Henry as duke of Normandy even though it cost them further concessions in the Norman Vexin. It took three unexpected twists of fortune to transform the position from one of a delicate balance of power to one in which Henry enjoyed a clear preponderance.

The first of these events was the premature death of Geoffrey, not yet 40, in September 1151. Had he lived long enough to see Henry crowned king at Westminster, the count would have been able to carry out his plan of leaving Anjou to his second son Geoffrey. But if this plan was now put into immediate effect then Henry, with only the resources of Normandy to call upon, would have much less chance of wresting England out of Stephen's grasp. So, according to the story first told in the 1190s by William of Newburgh, the dying Geoffrey decided that Henry should have both his paternal as well as his maternal inheritance on condition that he transfer Anjou to Geoffrey as soon as England had been conquered. In theory this was all very fair, but how could he ensure that Henry kept his side of the bargain? The best that the dying count could do was to give instructions that his body should not be buried until Henry had sworn a solemn oath to observe the terms of his father's will. When Henry, who had not been present at the deathbed, arrived for the funeral, he at first refused to take the oath but eventually, confronted by his father's decomposing body, he agreed to do so. For the moment his younger brother had to be content with the three castles of Chinon, Loudun and Mirebeau.

The second unexpected twist was Henry's marriage to another great heiress – Eleanor of Aquitaine. In March 1152 Louis VII and Eleanor were divorced. Eight weeks later she married again. The political consequences of this domestic rearrangement were momentous. The king of France was in the awkward position of a king overshadowed by his subject – a powerful subject now all the harder to challenge since the death of Count Theobald IV of Blois and Champagne earlier in the year had led to the partition of that great princely holding between three sons. Why, then, had Louis decided to divorce Eleanor? The king needed a son and after fourteen years of marriage, Eleanor had borne him only two daughters. Moreover, the couple were by now on such bad terms that further children were unlikely. In these circumstances divorce was sensible politics – so long as Louis could keep control of Aquitaine, which meant control of its duchess. Louis, however, was anything but a ruthless man and he seems to have made no effort to keep Eleanor under restraint either during or after the divorce proceedings. This, of course, did not prevent him being very angry when she married Henry Plantagenet. He at once set about organizing a grand coalition of all of Henry's rivals: King Stephen and his son Eustace (who was married to Louis VII's sister Constance); Count Henry of Champagne (as the man betrothed to Eleanor's elder daughter, his hopes of acquiring Aquitaine were threatened by the possibility of sons from the duchess's new marriage); Robert of Dreux, count of Perche (Louis VII's brother and a count whose county was strategically placed on the borders of Maine and Normandy); and finally, most sinister of all, Henry's own brother Geoffrey, who must have realized that a duke of Normandy married to the duchess of Aquitaine was unlikely ever to relinquish his hold on Anjou. In July 1152 Capetian troops attacked Aquitaine while Louis himself, together with Eustace, Henry and Robert, invaded Normandy and captured Neufmarché-sur-Epte. Geoffrey raised the standard of revolt in Anjou. In England Stephen took the initiative again and the Angevin loyalists there found they were hard put to defend themselves. According to Robert of Torigni the allies planned to deprive Henry of all his lands and divide them among themselves. Several Norman marcher lords, among them Hugh of Gournay, Hugh of Chateauneuf and Richer de L'Aigle, seeing which way the wind was blowing, renounced their allegiance. Informed opinion in Normandy, reported Robert of Torigni, was that Henry would not survive.

But the young prince's forays to England in the 1140s had made it abundantly clear that he in no way lacked courage and now, in the first real test of his political skill, he proved to be both resourceful and indomitable. The news of the invasion reached him when he was at Barfleur, about to embark for England. First he hurried across Normandy in order to see to the defence of the threatened eastern frontier, then he moved south to Anjou, besieging and capturing Montsoreau, a castle belonging to one of Geoffrey's supporters. This compelled Geoffrey to sue for peace. Fortunately for Henry, his enemies' attempt to take advantage of his absence from Normandy faltered when illness compelled King Louis to retire from the fray. Even so, his hold on his continental possessions remained a precarious one and his decision to sail to England in January 1153 impressed contemporaries by its sheer audacity. On the other hand, the risk to

Normandy and Anjou had to be balanced against the fact that his supporters in England had been pressing him to come to their aid for some years now. In 1151 and again in 1152 he had raised their hopes by making preparations to cross the Channel but had then been forced to disappoint them. If he wished to retain their loyalty he could not afford to go on like this. In these circumstances he had either to be bold or to resign himself to the loss of England. And why not resign England? After all he already ruled an immense principality stretching, as the annalist of Angers put it, 'from sea to sea' – from Normandy to Gascony, from the Channel to the Atlantic Ocean. But Henry was not the man to yield an inch of what he believed to be rightfully his. Boldness therefore it had to be.

Yet not even Henry's boldness was enough to break the deadlock. His defences on the continent held, but after seven months of continuous campaigning and political manoeuvring in England he had still failed to bring King Stephen to his knees. For this it required the third twist, the second unexpected death. In August 1153 Eustace died. Disheartened by this blow, which came not long after the death of a wife upon whom he had greatly relied, Stephen finally gave up the long struggle to keep the throne of England for the house of Blois. By the treaty of Winchester (November 1153) he recognized Henry as his heir in return for life possession of the throne and a guarantee that his second son, William, would be allowed to keep all his family lands in England and Normandy. In essence these were the same compromise peace terms that Henry of Blois had worked out in the spring of 1141 after the battle of Lincoln. The Empress Matilda's refusal to accept them then had condemned England to another 12 years of civil war. It is hardly surprising that Henry was welcomed in England as the bringer of peace when Stephen died in October 1154. For once the problem of the succession had been solved. Henry had no rivals for the throne of England; he could afford to take his time and deal first with unfinished business in Normandy. Not until 19 December 1154 was he crowned at Westminster – on the same Sunday as Stephen's coronation, perhaps to symbolize his position as Stephen's heir.

The acquisition of England meant the resurrection of the succession problem in Anjou itself. Now was the time for Henry to fulfil the terms of the oath sworn over his father's dead body. That oath had been made in September 1151 when Eleanor was still married to Louis VII. Whether or not Henry would have kept his promise had she remained so is an open question. What is clear is that once he had also acquired Aquitaine he would never relax his grip on the territories which served as the vital bridge connecting his mother's lands in the north and his wife's lands in the south. Hence within a few months of Henry's and Eleanor's wedding, his brother had joined the alliance against him. Geoffrey had been forced to submit then but now he had every justification for reminding his brother of the oath. The problem was eventually discussed at a family conference held at Rouen in February 1156. There Geoffrey learned that Henry had put this last year's grace to good use. He had sent an embassy including John of Salisbury to Rome and, from Adrian IV, the English pope, had received a dispensation. That troublesome oath had been sworn, he claimed, under duress and was therefore not binding.[5] All that Henry would do was offer his brother some compensation but, whatever it was, Geoffrey rejected it. He preferred instead to return to Anjou, there to fight for his right. Unfortunately for Geoffrey, although the moral basis for his claim may have been stronger after 1154 than it had been in 1152, his political position was a good deal weaker. Above all, he now had to do without the support of the most influential of his former allies: Louis VII. The king of France and Henry II had been reconciled since 1154 and, on the eve of the Rouen conference, Henry cemented their friendship by doing homage to Louis for Normandy, Anjou and Aquitaine. Having isolated his brother, Henry was able to crush his rebellion. After the fall of Chinon, Geoffrey's other strongholds (Loudun and Mirebeau) surrendered. In July 1156 he agreed to resign his claim to Anjou and accept just one lordship (Loudun) and an annual pension worth £1500 instead. Fortunately it was not long before Henry was able to improve his offer of compensation. Later in that same year the citizens of Nantes rebelled against their lord, Count Hoël, and appealed for Henry's help. It was given and, in return, Geoffrey was installed as the new count of Nantes. This was a notable acquisition, long sought after by the Angevins – as was made clear by Fulk IV's claim to be suzerain of Nantes. Whether or not Geoffrey would have been satisfied to remain just count of Nantes for long, we cannot say. He died in 1158 aged 24. Henry II's position as ruler of the Angevin inheritance was now beyond challenge.

---

5 For John of Salisbury, after his return from Rome, lamenting that he had gone further than was just in order to help Henry onto the throne of his fathers, see *The Letters of John of Salisbury. Volume One. The Early Letters*, (eds) W. J. Millor, H. E. Butler and C. N. L. Brooke (London, 1955), no. 19.

# 3 Aggression and expansion, 1156–72

It is customary to regard the defeat of Geoffrey Plantagenet in 1156 as marking the completion of the Angevin Empire. But that is not how Henry II saw it. So far as he was concerned there were still other inherited claims to pursue. His grandfather Henry I, building on the work of his predecessors, both Anglo-Saxon and Norman, had exercised some kind of suzerainty over neighbouring princes, suzerainty which both created a protective ring around England and Normandy and, at times, could provide scope for further expansion. The king of Scotland, the Welsh princes, the duke of Brittany and the counts of Perche and Flanders were the most important of these princes. Some of them, such as the counts of Perche and Flanders, were also subjects of the king of France, and in legal terms they owed allegiance to him; but by the end of Henry I's reign it was the king of England who was arranging their marriages for them – a sure sign of real lordship. By the time of Henry II's accession the protective ring had been well and truly breached. These princes had taken full advantage of the war of Norman succession to encroach on lands once ruled by Henry I.

King David of Scotland had taken Cumberland, Westmorland and Northumberland. In Wales two outstanding leaders had emerged, Rhys of Deheubarth and Owain of Gwynedd. At their hands the marcher lords in north and west had suffered both defeat and loss of territory. On the Continent there is no evidence that Norman overlordship was recognized by Eudo of Porhoët, duke of Brittany since 1148. In 1137 Stephen had granted two vital frontier castles, Moulins-la-Marche and Bonmoulins, to Rotrou III, count of Perche. Geoffrey Plantagenet was never in a position to recover them and after Rotrou's death in 1144, Louis VII gave the hand of the widowed countess to his own brother, Robert of Dreux. In 1153 Thierry, count of Flanders was also to be found in the French camp, helping Louis VII to wrest Vernon (controlling one of the strategically vital Seine bridges) out of Henry II's grasp. The loss of Vernon and Neufmarché in 1152–53 served as a reminder – if one were needed – of the menacing military consequences of the cession of the castles of the Norman Vexin in return for Louis VII's recognition of the Plantagenets as dukes of Normandy. Further south in the Loire valley, the old enemy, the count of Blois, had demanded Tours as the price of his acquiescence in the Angevin takeover of Normandy and, though he failed to obtain this, he did acquire the fortresses of Amboise and Fréteval. For Henry II, then, the task was not only to secure possession of his father's and grandfather's lands, but also to mend his fences. This meant the reassertion of the old suzerainties and, where possible, their intensification.

## FRANCE

In 1154 Louis VII allowed Henry to buy back Vernon and Neufmarché. This marked the beginning of a new stage in Angevin–Capetian relations. Louis recognized that his all-out effort of 1152–53 had failed to bring results commensurate with its costs and, after the Angevin acquisition of England in 1154, there could be no doubt that the military resources at his disposal fell far short of those which Henry could muster. In these circumstances peace was his best policy. But it was obvious that Henry would not rest until he had recovered the Norman Vexin. Agreement on this was reached after another demonstration of Angevin strength, an ostentatious display of apparently limitless wealth by Henry's chancellor, Thomas Becket, on the occasion of his visit to Paris in the summer of 1158. Margaret, Louis's first daughter by his second wife, Constance of Castile, was betrothed to Henry, Henry's eldest surviving son. Young Henry was three years old and Margaret was still a baby. But she was old enough to be assigned a dowry, the Norman Vexin. This was to be handed over when the marriage itself took place. In the meantime Margaret was to be kept in Henry's custody.

The policy of peace with France helped Henry to mend his frontiers elsewhere. Robert of Dreux was always under an obligation to yield Perche when Rotrou IV came of age but if there had been a state of war between Capetian and Angevin then Louis VII's belligerent brother might well have been reluctant to do so. Rotrou's succession to his county in 1158 was accompanied by Henry II's recognition of him as lord of the Norman seigneurie of

Bellême; in return Henry regained the former ducal castles of Moulins-la-Marche and Bonmoulins. At the same time Count Theobald of Blois agreed to restore Amboise and Fréteval. In 1162 Henry resumed possession of Gorron, Ambrières and Châtillon – castles which his parents had granted Juhel de Mayenne in 1135–36 (see p. 14).

## FLANDERS

In this harmonious atmosphere it had been relatively easy for Henry II to re-establish friendly relations with Thierry, count of Flanders. Not only were England and Flanders bound together by the wool trade but Thierry's wife, Sibylla of Anjou, was Henry's aunt. Count Thierry attended Henry's coronation as king of England in December 1154 and both count and countess were present at the important family conference at Rouen in February 1156 which discussed the question of Geoffrey's claim to Anjou. Next year, when Thierry and Sibylla went on a pilgrimage to Jerusalem they appointed Henry as guardian of their lands and of their heir Philip. The death, without issue, of William count of Mortain and Boulogne (King Stephen's second son) in 1159 enabled Henry to strengthen these family ties. He kept Mortain for himself but granted the honour of Boulogne, which included valuable manors around London and Colchester, together with the hand of Stephen's daughter Mary to Matthew, Thierry's younger son. Much of England's wool export passed through the count of Boulogne's port of Wissant on its way to the cloth manufacturing towns of Flanders so this was a marriage which made good sense in terms of commercial, as well as dynastic, politics. In order to carry out this plan Henry had had to haul Mary out of Romsey Abbey, where she was abbess. Common enough in the generation after the Norman Conquest, by the mid-twelfth century sending ex-nuns to the altar was altogether more extraordinary and shows just how highly Henry rated the Flemish connection. Flanders, like Wales, provided soldiers. One of the few diplomatic documents to survive from Henry II's reign is the text of the 1163 renewal of the traditional treaty between the post-conquest kings of England and the counts of Flanders. In return for a retainer of £500 a year, Thierry and Philip promised to provide 1000 knights on demand. Should Henry II be at war with Louis VII, the count of Flanders was entitled to perform the service due (20 knights) to the king of France, but the remainder of the thousand were to serve the king of England.

## BRITTANY

Eudo of Porhoët owed his position as duke to his marriage to the previous duke's daughter Bertha. She already had a son, Conan, the child of her first marriage to Alan of Brittany, a Breton count who was also earl of Richmond. In 1148 Conan had been a minor but once he was old enough to take possession of Richmond there can be no doubt that he then became Henry II's ideal candidate for the duchy: a duke of Brittany with valuable estates in England was a duke over whom the king of England had an obvious hold. In these circumstances it is very difficult indeed to believe that Henry II did not have a hand in the disturbances in Brittany in the autumn of 1156 – disturbances which led to Conan replacing Eudo as duke and Geoffrey Plantagenet replacing Hoël as count of Nantes. There followed a seemingly inexorable process of intensification of the Angevin suzerainty over Brittany. In 1158 Geoffrey died and Henry himself took over Nantes, though he first of all had to muster a massive army at Avranches in order to frighten Conan off. Increasingly over the next few years he behaved as though he were lord of Brittany, or at any rate of eastern Brittany, arranging Conan's marriage, appointing an archbishop of Dol and manipulating to his own advantage the inheritance customs of the Breton nobles. Since there was no tradition of a strong ducal regime in Brittany no one liked this, neither Conan nor the nobles. Inevitably there was resistance to which Henry's response was to send in the troops. At the end of his first invasion, in 1166, he betrothed Conan's daughter to his son Geoffrey. He then forced Conan to resign in favour of his future son-in-law, in effect to Henry himself since Geoffrey was only seven years old (the marriage between him and Constance of Brittany did not take place until 1181). Not surprisingly this high-handed behaviour provoked further opposition. More invasions followed, in 1167, 1168 and 1173. Only massive stone castles could have halted such hammerblows and these the Breton nobles could not afford. After the invasions came confiscations, measures which served to place still greater power in the hands of Henry and his agents, primarily William FitzHamo (until 1172) and Rolland of Dinan (from 1175 until Geoffrey himself took over in 1181). Brittany was being forced into the Angevin mould.

## SCOTLAND

In May 1157 Henry met King Malcolm IV (1153–65) at Chester and demanded the return of the northern counties to the English crown. In 1149 he had promised Malcolm's grandfather that all the land north of Newcastle and the Tyne should belong to the kings of Scotland for ever. But that was in 1149, when Henry's political position had been a weak one. There is no evidence that Henry had secured a papal dispensation from that oath but doubtless he reflected that he would not have sworn had he not been at a disadvantage. Now it was the young king of Scotland who was at a disadvantage so, as William of Newburgh put it, 'prudently considering that it was the king of England who had the better of the argument by reason of his much greater power', Malcolm gave way and did homage as required. In return he was granted the earldom of Huntingdon as King David had held it. He seems to have performed his military obligations to the full, accompanying Henry on expeditions to Toulouse in 1159 and against the Welsh in 1165. Given his own oath-breaking it is hardly surprising that Henry distrusted the Scots. When Malcolm renewed homage in 1163 he was also compelled to hand over hostages, including his youngest brother, David. The distrust deepened under Malcolm's successor William (1165–1214). Since King David had granted Northumbria to William in 1152, the new king had a very real grievance. By 1168 he was listed among Henry's enemies. In 1173 he took advantage of Henry's troubles to demand the restoration of Northumbria. When Henry refused, William invaded in 1173 and again in 1174. But for him the war ended in disaster. He was captured near Alnwick and in 1174 forced to accept the humiliating Treaty of Falaise. By its terms Edinburgh, Roxburgh, Jedburgh and Berwick, the key castles of Lothian, were handed over to English garrisons to be paid for out of Scottish revenues. As the Melrose Chronicler wrote, Scotland was now 'under a heavy yoke of domination and servitude' and remained so until the end of Henry II's reign.

## WALES

In 1157 Henry had been able to browbeat young Malcolm IV but Owain of Gwynedd and Rhys of Deheubarth (the Lord Rhys) were well-established princes and Wales was a very different kettle of fish.

It took three invasions (Gwynedd in 1157 and Deheubarth in 1158 and 1163) to persuade the Welsh princes to answer Henry's summons to court. But the terms which he imposed at Woodstock in July 1163 were harsh enough to move the Welsh to settle their own differences and unite against him. Henry's response to the revolt of 1164 was to invade again, this time on a massive scale. According to the Welsh *Chronicle of the Princes*, in 1165 Henry gathered 'a mighty host of the picked warriors of England and Normandy and Flanders and Anjou and Gascony and Scotland' (a catalogue which omitted the fleet hired from the Norse of Dublin) and his purpose was 'to carry into bondage and to destroy all the Britons'. The Welsh were saved by torrential summer rain. Frustrated and angry, Henry retreated and then had 22 Welsh hostages mutilated, girls as well as boys. After the disaster of 1165 the king's attitude to the Welsh princes was more circumspect. His invasion of Ireland in 1171–72 was a further reason for him to come to terms with the Lord Rhys, and his reward was the latter's loyalty during the crisis of 1173–74. Though with some alarms, as when Seisyll ap Dyfnwal of Gwent, together with his wife and young son, were murdered at Abergavenny in 1175, a sort of peace survived until 1183–84 when Henry's acquisition of the lordships of Glamorgan and Gower and hence the threat of direct crown rule in this region provoked Lord Rhys and his kin into a series of assaults on English castles in south Wales. Peace with the Welsh was always fragile, but it was more sensible than confrontation. Among its rewards was the fact that it gave the king of England better access to reserves of Welsh knife- and bowmen whose military expertise in wooded and hilly terrain made them masters of guerrilla warfare and the terror of their employer's continental enemies.

In northern France and in Britain Henry II recovered – and more than recovered – all the territories and rights which had been claimed by his ancestors. But Henry went further yet, and in two directions: Ireland and Toulouse.

## IRELAND

Henry's phenomenal success in the years 1152–54 had encouraged him to consider plans for further expansion. His youngest brother William was as yet unprovided for and since Henry was unwilling to give up any of his own patchwork inheritance, fresh fields would have to be conquered. During the autumn of 1155 Henry toyed with the idea of conquering Ireland. The country's state of political fragmentation made it a tempting target, while its conquest could be easily justified. To laymen it would appear that Henry II was only doing what King Arthur was said to have done and what William the Conqueror had dreamed of. The papacy was likely to bless an enterprise which would bring the Irish Church into line with the rest of Latin Christendom. The embassy which was sent to Rome to secure the king's dispensation from the oath over his father's body was also instructed to obtain Adrian IV's approval for the conquest of Ireland. That approval was forthcoming. In the words of the bull *Laudabiliter,* 'Laudably and profitably does your magnificence contemplate extending your glorious name on earth'. Yet by the time the embassy returned armed with the best rhetoric which the papal chancery could provide, his magnificence had decided to postpone his Irish expedition for a while. Presumably there were other problems nearer at home, most likely Geoffrey's claim to Anjou, which required his attention. With so many territories to rule there always were other problems. William died in 1164, still unprovided for. Although the idea of a conquest of Ireland faded into the background, Henry continued to regard the island as being within his sphere of influence. Thus in 1167 when King Dermot of Leinster came to him for help he was ready enough to describe him as 'prince of the men of Leinster, our vassal and liegeman' and give him permission to recruit allies and soldiers in England and Wales.

Armed with this licence Dermot was eventually able to persuade a marcher lord, Richard Fitz Gilbert – known as 'Strongbow' – plus a group of his friends and kinsmen, to try their luck in Ireland. Richard Fitz Gilbert's price was Dermot's daughter in marriage and, with her, the succession to her father's kingdom. In September 1170 the newcomers captured Dublin. The news of their swift success alarmed Henry and when he heard of Dermot's death (in May 1171), he reacted quickly. By October he had landed a large army near Waterford. Recognizing the mailed fist when they saw it, most of the native kings of Ireland attended his court and did homage. By 1175 even Rory O'Connor, the king of Connacht who claimed to be High King, had been persuaded to recognize Henry II's overlordship and pay a tribute measured in cattle hides. So far as Henry was concerned the kingdom of Ireland now belonged to him and his heirs. He confirmed Strongbow in his possession of Leinster, gave Meath to Hugh de Lacy and kept the old Norse centres of Dublin,

Waterford and Wexford to be governed by royal officials. The rest of the country remained in Irish hands, but this did not prevent Henry from granting other – as yet unconquered – kingdoms, Cork, Limerick and Ulster to English courtiers, to see what they could make of them. In 1180 Laurence O'Toole, the last Irish archbishop of Dublin, died and was replaced by a royal chancery clerk, John Comyn. 'Celtic' Ireland was being transformed into an Anglo-Irish province of the Angevin Empire. In the 1190s, in a chapter entitled 'The Conquest of the Irish by the English', William of Newburgh observed that 'a people who had been free since time immemorial, unconquered even by the Romans, a people for whom liberty had seemed an inborn right, were now fallen into the power of the king of England'.

Ireland's role in Henry's scheme of things was made plain in 1177 when he announced that his nine-year-old youngest son was to be the new province's lord. Not until 1185 was John old enough actually to take possession of his princely lordship. Then the young man's expedition was a fiasco. John returned to England before the end of the year, blaming others for his failure. He had alienated the Irish and failed to bring the ambitious Hugh de Lacy to heel. In this, as in other ways, a pattern had been set. Another 25 years were to elapse before John next set foot in Ireland. Under the formal lordship of an absentee prince, shielded by the umbrella of Angevin power, the speculative developers came over from England, built their castles and took their profits.

## TOULOUSE

Henry's marriage to Eleanor of Aquitaine meant that the rights and claims of her ancestors also needed to be considered: above all their claim to the county of Toulouse. In view of its wealth and strategic importance, Toulouse was a prize well worth having. It was also likely to be a tough nut to crack. Toulouse was an exceptionally large and well-fortified city and its ruler, Count Raymond V, was married to Louis VII's sister. Henry's new policy of peace with France was in part designed to detach Louis from his brother-in-law of Toulouse. The army which marched south from Poitiers in June 1159 was probably the largest he ever mustered. While he approached Toulouse from the north, his allies, the Trencavels and the count of Barcelona – ancient enemies of the house of Toulouse – advanced towards the city from the south. In the event Louis chose to stand by Raymond. Their determined resistance ensured that the city itself did not fall but both Henry and his allies made substantial territorial gains at Raymond's expense, castles in the valley of the Garonne and, above all, Cahors and its surrounding region, the Quercy.

The expedition of 1159 marked the beginning of what William of Newburgh was to call a 'forty years' war' against Toulouse. Henry campaigned in this region in 1161; after that, though he himself became preoccupied elsewhere, his servants, including the archbishop of Bordeaux in 1164, and his allies, notably Alfonso II of Aragon, kept up the military pressure. In 1171 Henry entered into negotiations with Count Humbert of Maurienne, another of Raymond V's enemies, and two years later negotiations culminated in the betrothal of Prince John to the count's daughter. Three weeks later, at a court held at Limoges (25 February 1173), Raymond gave way at last. In the presence of the kings of Aragon and Navarre he knelt and did homage for the county of Toulouse, first to Henry II, then to his eldest son Henry, and finally to Richard who had been installed as duke of Aquitaine in the previous year.

Henry's attitude towards Toulouse stands in marked contrast to his treatment of the Pyrenean region. The history of Gascony furnished sufficient grounds on which he could have pushed claims to lordship over Béarn, Bigorre, Comminges, Armagnac and Fezensac. But he seems to have made no effort to do so; indeed he allowed Béarn to slip into the orbit of Aragon and stay there. His attitude to the southernmost part of his dominions is plainly revealed by the terms on which he gave his daughter Eleanor in marriage to Alfonso VIII of Castile in 1170. Her dowry was to be nothing less than Gascony itself (see p. 32). Henry had no intention of disinheriting his wife; the gift was to be handed over only after Eleanor of Aquitaine's death. In due course the marriage treaty of 1170 was to add not a little to John's troubles, but in the meantime Henry's policy of friendship with the powers of Christian Spain was calculated to bring about the diplomatic isolation of Toulouse.

## THE END OF THE ANGEVIN–CAPETIAN ACCORD

The invasion of Toulouse had made it clear to Louis that, so far as Henry was concerned, peace with France was not part of a general peace, simply an opportunity to make war elsewhere. Louis's love of peace impressed all of his contemporaries but, as king of the French, he could not honourably stand by while men who were his subjects and kinsmen were attacked. Thus 1159 marked the end of the brief interlude of Angevin–Capetian friendship. When Constance of Castile (Louis's second wife) died in childbirth in 1160, and Louis announced that he was going to remarry at once, Henry responded by having young Henry and Margaret married. Immediately after the ceremony, in November 1160, the castles of the Norman Vexin were transferred to Henry's lordship. Although the wedding had been legalized by papal dispensation, it is clear that Henry had broken the spirit of the 1158 treaty and Louis was correspondingly angry. But why had Henry reacted sharply to the news of Louis's forthcoming remarriage? Partly, perhaps, because the French king's intended bride was Adela of Champagne and the match meant a renewal of the worrying alliance between the houses of Blois-Champagne and Capet. Partly, perhaps, because any remarriage increased Louis's chances of producing a son and if, in the absence of a male heir, there were to be a Capetian succession crisis, who could tell who might be the next king of France? It is hard to believe that, in these tempting circumstances, Henry would not have pushed the claims of his eldest son – and who could push harder than Henry II?

From now on the two kings were at odds on almost every issue of secular and ecclesiastical politics. Throughout the 1160s and 1170s Henry continued to press every conceivable claim against Louis VII – and some that to a less creative brain than Henry's must have seemed inconceivable. At times Henry's claims were probably meant only to keep Louis on the diplomatic defensive, but at other times he resorted to force of arms. The most blatant example of this was the coup by which he attempted to seize Bourges in 1170. Bourges was strategically vital and as the chief city of Berry it lay in a region in which the duke of Aquitaine had some interests (mostly in the Châteauroux district in the west of Berry) and to which he could advance claims with some slight degree of plausibility. Henry argued that the archbishopric of Bourges belonged by right to Aquitaine: this also had the effect of strengthening his claim over Auvergne, a region into which he marched an army in 1167, compelling Louis to respond by raiding the Vexin to draw him back north. When Louis VII rushed south to save Bourges in 1170 he must have wondered whether there was ever going to be an end to Henry's aggressively expansionist policies.

## THE KING'S CHILDREN

Did Henry II have an overriding purpose? It is most unlikely to have been 'empire-building' in the sense of consciously putting together a political structure which was intended to survive its creator's death. As we have already seen in the cases of Ireland and Brittany, the arrangements which Henry made for his conquests suggest that, in so far as he looked to the future at all, it was in terms of providing for his children. The arrangements made for the other parts of the empire fit into this basically dynastic framework. In 1169 Henry announced that Anjou, Normandy and England should go to Henry, his eldest surviving son, leaving Aquitaine for Richard, the second son.

Kings also, of course, had to make provision for their daughters. If they did not wish to become an abbess – and by the late twelfth century it was not as easy to push an unwilling woman into a nunnery as it once had been – they would usually be given in marriage, together with a cash dowry, to a neighbouring prince. Thereafter the costs of supporting them were borne by their husband's family. This is what happened to Matilda (born 1156; married to Henry the Lion, duke of Bavaria and Saxony in 1168) and to Joan (born 1165; married to King William II of Sicily in 1177). The marriage settlement of Eleanor (born 1161) was, however, a much more remarkable one: she and her husband, King Alfonso VIII of Castile, were to have the duchy of Gascony (see above, p. 30). Henry II, in other words, treated his lands not as a single, unified 'state' but as a partible family estate, as had his own father before him (see above p. 18). As it happened, in the next generation things turned out differently but, in certain circumstances, they might not have done. The treaties which Richard (at Messina, in March 1191) and John (at Paris, in January 1194) made with Philip Augustus both envisaged some kind of partition in the event of them having two or more heirs.

Some of Henry's arrangements took effect, up to a point at any rate, during the old king's lifetime: the young Henry was crowned king of England in 1170 and Richard installed as duke of Aquitaine in 1172. In 1181 Brittany was handed over to Geoffrey, though his father retained Nantes until 1185. (For John and Ireland, see p. 29.) There were several advantages to this custom. It tended to diminish quarrels about who should get what after the ruler's death. It gave young men some early experience of government. And in the case of dominions as extensive as Henry II's it meant that the presence of the king's sons in different parts of the empire might have helped to provide the mobility, flexibility and speed of response which he alone, despite his phenomenal energy, could not give. In 1177 he is reported to have said that he, when alone, had yielded none of his rights and that it would be a disgrace if they were to lose anything now that there were several of them to rule. There were, of course, costs to this policy. A young and ambitious man ruling one province might not always agree with his father's priorities and might well resent being overruled. Richard in Aquitaine or Geoffrey in Brittany might have a relatively free hand for much of the time; but for the young king, as designated heir to the ancestral lands, there was the greater frustration of living more or less permanently in his father's shadow. Whatever policy was adopted it was always likely that there would be tensions within the dynasty. As Henry's sons grew older, so there would be increasing scope for the king of France to make life difficult for his overbearing neighbour.

# 4 Holding on, 1173–99

## THE REBELLION OF 1173–74 AND ITS AFTERMATH

Louis VII's opportunity came in the spring of 1173. Henry betrothed his five-year-old youngest son, John, to the heiress to the county of Maurienne and announced that he would provide for him by giving him three castles in Anjou: Chinon, Loudun and Mirebeau. This offended the 18-year-old Young King. He had still not been assigned any lands from which he could maintain himself and his queen in their proper estate. Angrily he demanded that at least part of his inheritance, England or Normandy or Anjou, should be handed over to him at once. The Old King refused – he was, after all, not yet 40 himself. He insisted that his oldest son should remain at court with him, but one night the Young King slipped away and rode to the court of his mother's ex-husband and his own father-in-law, Louis VII. That there should be tension between Henry II and the designated heir to his ancestral lands, was only to be expected. What was unexpected, indeed shocking, was that Henry's wife Eleanor would join the revolt against her husband, and would send Richard and Geoffrey to join their brother at the court of France. It was only natural that those neighbouring princes who had suffered at Henry's hands should seize the opportunities presented by the family crisis. Hence the revolt of Henry's wife and sons triggered a greater war, involving the kings of France and Scotland, the counts of Flanders, Boulogne and Blois, as well as a sprinkling of rebels in Poitou, Normandy and England. In the end, Henry emerged victorious. He won on the continent partly because he captured Eleanor at an early stage in the war, and partly because, as the richest king in western Europe, he had the cash resources which enabled him to hire mercenaries – usually known as Brabançons or routiers – on a scale which his enemies could not match. In Britain he owed his victory to the capture of the king of Scots in 1174 (see above p. 26). But though he won, the events of 1173–74 revealed the chink in Henry's political armour, his inability to manage his own family, and they provided the first indications that he would have to struggle to hold on to what he had.

Naturally there was at first no sign that Henry himself saw it this way. After 1174 he kept Eleanor in prison but reinstated his sons and continued to press on. In 1177 he bought the county of La Marche, a purchase that strengthened his hold on eastern Aquitaine. In the same year he claimed that Louis VII had agreed to include the French Vexin in the dowry which he bestowed upon his daughter Margaret when she married the Young King. This, he asserted, should be handed over at once. On the same occasion he claimed Bourges – a city which had long been firmly attached to the French crown – on the grounds, seemingly entirely fictional, that it had been settled upon another of Louis VII's daughters, Alice, when she had been betrothed to Richard eight years earlier in 1169. But, in contrast to his earlier conduct he no longer followed up his claims with military action. After the invasion of Ireland in 1171–72 he launched no further attacks on his neighbours. As he grew older, the rigours of campaigning became harder to take. In 1180 he fell seriously ill. By the late 1180s he was said by William of Newburgh to be 'sick to death of war'. After 1172 his campaigns were defensive ones, and for the sake of peace he was willing to make concessions. In 1186 he returned Edinburgh to William of Scotland. The aggressive young Henry of the 1150s and 1160s, Henry II Part One, became a peace-loving king who devoted himself to hunting and government: Henry II Part Two. On the whole, it is the latter who is the Henry familiar to us from history books. 'Few people', as Antonia Gransden observed, 'wrote history in the first half of Henry II's reign.'[1] But English historical writing saw a notable revival during the 1170s and the 1180s, and of this new generation of historians, the two best known, Roger of Howden and Ralph of Diceto, happened to share a common interest in the country's administration. This late twelfth-century development, coupled with the fashion for constitutional and administrative history that dominated so much of the nineteenth and twentieth centuries, meant that Henry II Part One would vanish almost completely behind the image of the lawyer-king of Part Two.

---

1 A. Gransden, *Historical Writing in England* c. 550 to c. 1307 (London, 1974), p. 219.

## PHILIP II AUGUSTUS

If the coming of age of his own sons posed problems for Henry II, they were relatively minor compared with the problems that were to be caused for him and for his successors by the coming of age of Louis VII's son. Only 15 when his father died in 1180, at the start of his reign Philip II owed much to the assistance given him by Henry and his sons. But he developed rapidly. Already by 1183 he had embarked on the policy that was to defeat Henry II in 1188–89, and bring the Angevin Empire to its knees. By the 1190s his territorial gains had led to him being called Philip Augustus. By the end of a long reign (1223) he had proved to be the most successful king in French history. Central to this success was his policy of using the Angevins against themselves. He began by setting out to undermine Henry where he had already shown himself to be vulnerable, in the management of his own family, and he pursued this policy systematically, employing, one after the other, his sons against the Old King, then John against his brother Richard, and Arthur of Brittany against his uncle John. When the supply of disgruntled Angevin princes ran dry, Philip turned to his own son, Louis, by then married to Henry II's grand-daughter, Blanche of Castile, and set him to invade King John's England in 1216. By this date Philip had driven the Angevins out of Anjou and Normandy and had established himself as the master of a greater kingdom of France. With the advantage of hindsight Gerald de Barri drew a word picture of Philip at a council meeting of his barons at the start of his reign, sitting apart from them, chewing on a hazel stick, apparently lost to the world. When asked what was on his mind, the young and still untried king replied that he had been wondering whether it would be given to him to make France great again, as it had been in the days of Charlemagne.

## THE OLD KING AND RICHARD

Philip II's first opportunity came in 1183. From 1175 onwards Henry II had increasingly left the government of Aquitaine to Richard, but the latter's imperious and all too effective political style caused resentment in the traditionally more independent parts of the duchy: the Angoumois, Limousin and Périgord. According to Roger of Howden, among the wrongs which Richard was accused of inflicting on his subjects was his custom 'of carrying off their wives, daughters and kinswomen, making them his concubines, then passing them on to his soldiers when he had sated his own lust on them'. In 1183 the Young King, egged on by Geoffrey of Brittany who had recently been quarrelling violently with his father, decided to join a rebellion led by the viscount of Limoges and Geoffrey of Lusignan. Their plan was to unseat Richard as duke of Aquitaine and replace him with his more malleable older brother Henry. But Richard had been carrying out his father's policies and so the Old King marched to Limoges to support him against his two brothers and their local allies. As the internecine war came to the boil in the Limousin, Philip saw his chance. He sent troops to support the Young King, as did Raymond V of Toulouse and the duke of Burgundy. For a few weeks in the early summer of 1183 Henry II and Richard looked to be in difficulties, but in June they were rescued by the Young King's sudden fatal illness.

His older brother's death meant that Richard was now promoted to the position of principal heir. In consequence it also meant that he inherited his brother's legacy of tense relations with their father. Later that same year Henry ordered Richard to hand Aquitaine to John (who was already known as Lackland) in return for the latter's homage. On the face of it, a reasonable arrangement, since Richard could now look forward to ruling England, Normandy and Anjou; none the less he refused to comply. He had not worked and fought for the last eight years building up his own ducal authority in Aquitaine in order to give it away. He knew that it was only his possession of Aquitaine that prevented him from being just as humiliatingly dependent on his father as the Young King had been. The Old King now discovered that he had met his match. It was not only that Richard had already won a considerable reputation as a soldier. It was also the fact that since he rather than his father had been in charge of the day-to-day management of patronage and government in Aquitaine since 1175, he had built up political ties that would now take the Old King a great deal of time and effort to undo – as he would have to if he were to compel Richard to relinquish the duchy. But the Old King had many other calls on his time. Some Welsh princes were in revolt; the king of Scots was pressing for return of his castles; most awkward of all, King Philip was demanding that now that the Young King was dead his widow's marriage portion – the Norman Vexin – should be returned. Henry II could – and did – look to Geoffrey and John to put military pressure on

Richard, but faced with these competing demands upon his attention, that was as far as he felt able to go. It was not far enough. By 1185 he was reduced to the face-saving tactic of asking Richard to surrender the duchy not to him but to Eleanor, the lawful duchess – in effect an admission that Aquitaine remained Richard's portion. Next year Henry supplied Richard with the resources to mount a campaign against Raymond of Toulouse, probably to re-assert an Aquitanian control over the Quercy that had been lost in the family crisis of 1183. The continuing rancour between Richard and Geoffrey, however, had alerted Philip Augustus to the Breton duke's potential as an instrument of Capetian policy. Geoffrey's presence at Philip's court led to all manner of rumours about their intentions but, whatever they were, they were brought to nothing by Geoffrey's death in a tournament in August 1186.

Philip Augustus, undaunted by the loss of both the Young King and Geoffrey, now turned his mind to Richard. In June 1187 Henry II was deeply alarmed, so it was reported, when he heard that Richard and Philip 'were eating at the same table, sharing the same dish, sharing the same bed'. This was not sex – as some twentieth-century authors used to imagine – but, as contemporaries realized, a very public political gesture. Proclaiming themselves to be close allies who trusted each other, Richard and Philip were defying Henry. How had it come to this after the reconciliation signalled by the 1186 Toulouse campaign? What had made Richard decide to share Philip's bed?

Sex probably did come into it. Not between Richard and Philip, but between Richard's father and Richard's fiancée. She had been betrothed to Richard in 1169 and had been handed over to the Old King's custody – where she had stayed ever since. By 1176 her father Louis VII was becoming concerned by the fact that she was still not married. From then on virtually every round of negotiations between the kings of England and France ended by confirming her betrothal – yet still she remained unmarried and in Henry's custody. According to Gerald de Barri, in 1187 Henry had written to Philip suggesting that Alice should marry John instead. Philip – naturally – sent the letter to Richard. 'From that hour onwards', wrote Gerald, 'Richard suspected that his father was planning to disinherit him and hated him.' No such letter is known to exist, indeed it is improbable that such a proposal would ever have been committed to ink and parchment. In 1183, however, Henry had promised Philip that he would grant the Norman Vexin to whichever of his sons married Alice. This was an open-ended formula which created fertile ground for any subsequent rumour that the Old King was intending to promote John at Richard's expense – and after the fiasco of John's expedition to Ireland in 1185 (see above p. 29), it did seem plausible that he would try to provide for him on the Continent.

More damaging still was the rumour that Henry had seduced the young princess entrusted to him. Philip raised the question of her marriage in 1183, 1186, 1187, 1188, and 1189. Eventually in 1191 Richard was to tell Philip that he could prove that Alice had had a son by his father, and the king of France, deeply humiliated, was forced to drop his insistence that his sister marry Richard. The seduction of Alice was a further complication in the already complicated relationships between Henry, Philip and Richard, and presumably Gerald was at least right in thinking that her situation played its part in the 1187 breach between father and son. Probably already, certainly at the latest by 1188, Richard had no intention of marrying Alice, and had found himself another fiancée, though he managed to conceal this from Alice's brother – his vitally important ally – until 1190. (Alice was eventually restored to Philip in 1195 and was promptly married to the count of Ponthieu, lord of Eu and Tréport, one of Philip's allies in his invasion of Normandy.)

In 1187 it did not take long before Henry and Richard were formally reconciled once again, but equally it was not long before new tensions emerged. In that same autumn Richard took the cross. Of all the rulers north of the Alps he was the first to respond to the news of Saladin's capture of Jerusalem in October 1187 – the news that shocked all Christendom and led to the launching of the Third Crusade. The scale of the shock is shown by the way even such reluctant crusaders as Henry II and Philip were forced by public opinion to follow his example. Most contemporaries admired the speed and decisiveness of Richard's response, but he had acted without consulting his father, and his father was stunned. Yet again the two were publicly reconciled soon enough, but this was clearly a relationship close to the end of its tether. In 1188 Richard found himself simultaneously facing aggression from Raymond V of Toulouse and rebellion by the Lusignans and the count of Angoulême; according to rumour both internal and external opponents had received financial support from Henry. No contemporary historian was more sympathetic to the Old King than the dean of St Paul's, Ralph Diceto – yet rather than suppress this rumour, he identified it as the cause of the final breach between son and father. On both fronts Richard was victorious. He put down the rebellion and carried the war against Count Raymond right up to the gates of Toulouse. Then he went north to help his father defend their dominions against Philip's attacks – but too late to be able to prevent the king of France adding the important Berry stronghold of Châteauroux to the gains (Issoudun and Graçay) he had already made in that region in the previous year.

In November 1188 at Bonmoulins, where the two kings met to discuss peace, Henry publicly refused to recognize Richard as his heir. According to Gervase of Canterbury, he spoke 'evasively as was his custom'. 'Now at last,' said Richard, 'I must believe what I had always thought was impossible.' Then and there he did homage to Philip for all the lands which his father held of the king of France. After a short truce, and now with Richard fighting on his side, the king of France's war against the king of England was renewed. In the view of the author of the *Histoire de Guillaume le Maréchal* writing in the 1220s, this marked the beginning of a long, and in the end disastrous, war. Henry found no support in Aquitaine. The Bretons rose in revolt against a king who had done so much to limit their independence. By March 1189 the Old King was ill. By promising to abide by arbitration he obtained a truce, but when he rejected the terms offered at a Whitsun peace conference, Richard and Philip invaded Maine and the Touraine. Henry's position collapsed. In June his birthplace Le Mans surrendered. On 3 July Tours, the strategic key to the Angevin dominions in France, fell. Next day the dying king met Philip and Richard and acquiesced in the terms which they dictated. He agreed to pay Philip 20,000 marks and promised that all his subjects, both in England and on the continent, would be made to swear an oath of allegiance to Richard as his acknowledged heir. Two days later the Old King died in misery, knowing that in the end he had been defeated, and that John had joined the winning side. In the eyes of contemporary moralists, both French and English, the misery was the price he had to pay for his part in the murder of Becket.

## RICHARD I: GOING ON CRUSADE

From his father's funeral at Fontevraud Richard sent instructions to England, ordering his mother's release from the surveillance under which Henry had once again placed her. Anticipating that the Welsh would take up arms as soon as they heard of the Old King's death, he also sent an envoy to Wales to try to keep the peace. His chosen envoy was Gerald de Barri, cousin of the Lord Rhys of Deheubarth, but the task was difficult, perhaps impossible. Gerald did not succeed. Rhys made some gains and laid siege to Carmarthen, beginning a campaign of recovery in south-west Wales that would continue for several years. Eleanor, on the other hand, succeeded in what was a much easier task, ensuring that Richard would be given an enthusiastic reception on his arrival in England. On 13 September 1189 he was crowned king in Westminster Abbey. After all the anxieties in the end it turned out to be the first time for centuries that in England a son had succeeded, without dispute, to his father's crown. By this time, of course, Richard had been installed as duke of Normandy and had come to terms with the king of France. Once again Philip claimed the Norman Vexin, but dropped his demand when Richard, yet again, expressed his willingness to marry Alice. Although Philip restored Châteauroux, Richard recognized Philip's lordship over Graçay and Issoudun and acknowledged that Auvergne more properly belonged to the crown of France than to the duchy of Aquitaine. In order to meet Philip's expenses he added another 4,000 to the 20,000 marks which Henry had promised. John remained lord of Ireland, under Richard's overlordship. There had been some crumbling at the edges, in south-west Wales and in Berry, but otherwise Richard had inherited the whole of his father's empire intact. Given the many plans to partition the lands in 1169 and later it was in many ways a very surprising outcome of the past 20 years of politics.

Richard's overriding priority was now the crusade. Contemporaries were unanimous in believing this was his highest duty, primarily a religious duty, but not only that. The events of 1128 (see p. 11) had brought Jerusalem as well as England and Normandy within the Angevin orbit. If the Angevin Empire was a family firm, then the kingdom of Jerusalem was an outlying branch. Queen Sibylla of Jerusalem was a cousin. As she and her husband – Guy of Lusignan, one of Richard's Poitevin subjects – fought to save their tottering kingdom, it was the family duty of the head of the senior branch of the family, first Henry II, now Richard I, to do what they could to help. By 1189 the attention of the whole Latin Christian world was fixed on the siege of Acre, where a crusading force besieging the Muslim garrison was itself hemmed in by Saladin's field army. The politics of 1188–89 had already caused delays enough, and it was time to move. That the prolonged absence of the ruler on crusade would create problems was obvious. They just had to be faced.

One predictable problem was that his brother John would intrigue against him. There was little that could be done to prevent this. However, it was only in alliance with Philip Augustus that John's intrigues were likely to be dangerous, and that being so, it was better that John should stay behind, as far away from Philip as possible. In any event if Richard were to die on crusade, John was, for the moment at least, the most plausible heir. So Richard gave him the hand of Isabel, heiress to the earldom of Gloucester and lordship of Glamorgan, the county of Mortain in Normandy and an additional £4,000 a year worth of land in England. In doing this he carried out their father's express wishes. Writing with the benefit of hindsight, William of Newburgh asserted that Richard's fondness for John had led him to treat his younger brother with imprudent generosity, arguing that it only encouraged his ambition and tempted him into treachery. Whether John thought he had been treated generously is another matter. He may well have felt that in England and Normandy he had been given wealth but disproportionately little power. Other potential threats came from England's neighbours. As lord of Glamorgan it would be in John's interest to hold in check the ambitions of the Lord Rhys and his sons. In September 1189 Richard himself met other Welsh rulers at Worcester where they swore not to attack England while he was on crusade. In December he met William the Lion at Canterbury. In what is known as the Quitclaim of Canterbury, he acknowledged Scotland's independence, and restored Roxburgh and Berwick. In the words of the Melrose Chronicle, Scotland was freed 'from the heavy yoke of domination and servitude'. For this William paid 10,000 marks, a useful contribution to the crusade war chest.

But the first essential was to ensure that Philip went on crusade too. This meant that although Richard had evidently decided that he could not marry Alice, he could not afford to repudiate her either. Her brother would have reacted to such an insult to the honour of the French royal house with an immediate demand for massive territorial compensation and the threat of war. So to save the crusade he continued to give Philip the false impression that he would marry her on his return, even though he had already begun secret negotiations for another bride: Berengaria, daughter of King Sancho VI of Navarre. In 1188–89 an alliance with Navarre made good political sense. In the shock of 1187 only one ruler of a French principality did not take the cross: Raymond V of Toulouse, an old and still very active enemy of the house of Anjou. All the history of recent decades indicated that Raymond would grab the opportunity presented by the absence of the duke of Aquitaine. Diplomatic measures to protect the duchy's security were crucially important, and Richard did not go on crusade until the delicate negotiations that ensured that the king of Navarre would send troops to help in the event of trouble had been completed. Sancho's price was his daughter's marriage, and evidently he was unwilling to postpone this until after Richard's return – hardly surprising in view of what he already knew about Richard's treatment of Alice and Philip. So the extraordinary scheme was hatched whereby Richard went on crusade still betrothed to Alice, but then married Berengaria en route, presumably when it was judged that Philip was too far committed not to go on to Acre. Inevitably the Capetian king would be furious – but he was going to be one day anyway. In the meantime the plan at least secured an interval during which the crusade could go ahead, as well as helping to defend Aquitaine's frontiers. By the time Richard and Philip eventually rode out of Vézelay together at the start of their crusade (July 1190), everything that could have been done had been done.

## THE KING IN CAPTIVITY

The provisions for government in the king's absence worked well. On the Continent the seneschals of Normandy, Anjou, Poitou and Gascony did the jobs expected of them. In England Richard's chosen justiciar, William Longchamp, mishandled the problems created by Henry II's illegitimate son Geoffrey, whom Richard – again in accordance with their father's wishes – had made archbishop of York, and in 1191 his mistakes were skilfully exploited by John. In consequence Longchamp was driven from office, but – much to John's disappointment – he was replaced by Walter of Coutances, exactly as envisaged under contingency plans that Richard had already set in place. Philip Augustus's return from crusade subjected the system to a severe test. He had been angered by being forced to accept the repudiation of his sister in March 1191 and then humiliated by Richard's evident standing in the international limelight of the crusade as much the richer king and greater war-leader. He left as soon as possible after the capture of Acre. Rather than remain any longer in Richard's shadow he preferred to be blamed for abandoning the crusade – besides which, Count Philip of Flanders died at Acre in 1191 and, as many contemporaries cynically observed, Philip wanted to make sure that he got his share – Artois with the rich towns of Arras, Douai and St Omer – of the count's inheritance. He arrived back in France in time to spend Christmas 1191 at Fontainebleau. But the seneschal of Normandy, William FitzRalph – one of Henry II's old servants whom Richard kept in office – rejected Philip's territorial demands out of hand. Philip then invited John to Paris. In England it was believed that he offered to make John lord of all the Angevin lands in France if he would marry Alice – the fact that John already had a wife was evidently not a problem (see p. 90). However, the threat to confiscate all his estates in England if he accepted the invitation persuaded John to turn it down. In this respect at least Richard's generosity to John paid dividends. Philip tried to organize an invasion of Normandy, but it came to nothing since so many of his leading men refused to join an attack on the lands of an absent crusader. In the south the alliance with Navarre proved its worth. With Sancho of Navarre's help, the seneschal of Gascony, Elie de la Celle, was able to suppress rebellion and defeat the count of Toulouse (1192).

Richard himself left Palestine in October 1192, and should have been back in his own dominions by January 1193. Had he returned then, he would have found his lands intact. It would have been obvious to all that the provincial governments had coped extremely well. But in December 1192 he was captured by a Christian prince, Leopold of Austria, another of those alienated by Richard's imperious political style at Acre, and then handed over to the Emperor Henry VI. Throughout the whole of 1193 no one knew for sure when or whether Richard would be released. (One of his Norman predecessors, Robert Curthose, died in his brother's prison after spending nearly 30 years there.) Philip exploited this prolonged and unforeseeable crisis ruthlessly. Again he invited John to Paris and this time John went. In return for Philip's support and Alice's hand in marriage with Artois as her dowry, he promised to hand over the whole of the Norman Vexin. When he returned to England to stir up rebellion there, however, he won little support. Although he was able to hire some Welsh mercenaries, neither Welsh princes nor the king of Scotland joined his revolt. The precautionary measures which Richard had taken in 1189 proved their worth; besides, John's conduct was widely felt to be treacherous. Most remarkably of all,

William the Lion even made a contribution to Richard's ransom. In Aquitaine too a rebellion by Count Audemar of Angoulême was contained; indeed, the count himself fell into Elie de la Celle's hands.

But it was a different story in Normandy. Here Philip himself took charge of operations. Many of the lords of the Franco-Norman border threw in their lot with the king of France much as they had done when Henry II had been in trouble in 1173. On 12 April 1193 the castellan of the great Vexin fortress of Gisors betrayed his trust, opening the way for Philip to advance on Rouen. Although Philip was unable to press home his siege of the ducal capital, he obtained the rest of the Norman Vexin and much of eastern Normandy including Dieppe. He and his allies, Count Baldwin VIII of Flanders, Count Renaud of Boulogne and Count William of Ponthieu, now controlled all the ports from the Rhine to Dieppe and so posed a serious threat to the sea communications which were central to the very existence of the Anglo-Norman kingdom. In Normandy Richard's agents agreed to the Treaty of Mantes (July 1193), conceding Philip's right to keep all he had taken, and granting him four major strongholds, Drincourt and Arques in eastern Normandy, Loches and Châtillon-sur-Indre in the Touraine, as security for the 20,000 marks that they promised the king would pay Philip after his release. They felt they had no choice but to make terms with Philip in an attempt to stem the tide, and to give them a chance to raise the ransom demanded before Henry VI, determined to make maximum capital out of the situation, raised it still higher than he had already done – up from 100,000 to 150,000 marks. Despite his ally's triumphs on the continent, John's signal lack of success in England sent him running back to Paris. In a new treaty (in January 1194) he surrendered Tours and all the key castles of the Touraine; the whole of Normandy east of the Seine except for the city of Rouen and its environs; also Vaudreuil, Verneuil and Evreux; he granted Moulins and Bonmoulins to the counts of Perche, Vendôme to Louis of Blois; accepted the count of Angoulême's claim that his county was independent of the duchy of Aquitaine. So craven a treaty only made Philip despise John – an attitude that was to be of critical importance in 1199 and subsequently. Henry VI used the offers he received from Philip and John to make one further demand before he would release his prisoner. Richard must resign the kingdom of England to him, in order to receive it back as a fief of the empire. Eleanor had travelled to Mainz and on her advice Richard submitted to this final blackmail. In February 1194 he was at last released.

## RECOVERY: ADMINISTRATION, DIPLOMACY AND WAR

From now on the recovery of his lost territories was to be the political obligation which overrode all others. As William of Newburgh put it, 'It would have been dishonourable for the king of England to make peace given that his dominions had suffered so much at the hands of the king of France while he was in prison and in defiance of international law.' But his position was hardly promising. His subjects (not just in England but in all his dominions) had found the 100,000 marks necessary to obtain his release, but the sum of 50,000 marks was still outstanding and would have to be paid if his hostages were to be freed. He had admittedly made the best of his enforced stay in Germany by building up a coalition of allies headed by the archbishop of Cologne, the count of Holland, and the dukes of Brabant and Limburg. In time this Lower Rhineland coalition was to achieve its purpose: put pressure on the count of Flanders and so help to deprive Philip of his most important ally. But for the moment it represented a further charge on his financial resources. By contrast Philip's position was a strong one. The inheritance of prosperous lands in north-eastern France, the Amienois in 1185 and Artois in 1191–92, had made him a much richer ruler than his father had been. Indeed, it was for his territorial gains in this part of France that Rigord of St Denis named him Augustus. He was now powerfully placed in a region from which he could both increase the pressure on eastern Normandy and maintain closer contact with the immensely wealthy Count Baldwin, i.e. Baldwin V of Hainault who, as Baldwin VIII of Flanders, had taken over the greater part of the possessions of Count Philip. The king whose wealth on crusade, in Sicily and at Acre, had outshone Philip's, was now the poorer of the two.

Fortunately for Richard, England at least was secure, and could be left in the exceptionally capable hands of Hubert Walter, whose qualities as politician, diplomat and administrator he had witnessed on crusade and whose appointment as archbishop of Canterbury and as justiciar, he, still in prison, had secured in 1193. As archbishop of Canterbury Hubert Walter possessed authority over Welsh dioceses and he proved able to browbeat the Welsh. On his return to England, Richard took over John's lordship of Ireland, removing his justiciar and replacing him with John de Courcy and Walter de Lacy. This allowed William Marshal to take possession of the lordship of Leinster. Although Richard refused William the Lion's claim on the northern counties, he managed to do so in a way which kept the two kings on friendly terms. King William carried a sword before Richard at the ceremonial crown-wearing at Winchester (17 April 1194) which – against the homage he had sworn to the Emperor Henry VI – asserted the king's full recovery of sovereignty in England. It was a remarkable – and possibly unique – gesture of political friendship between the kings of England and Scotland. Next year William proposed that Richard's nephew Otto should marry his daughter Margaret and become heir-presumptive to the Scottish throne. In Scotland, Richard's reputation as 'that noble king so friendly to the Scots' was to survive even the Anglo-Scottish wars from Edward I's time onwards.

Described by Holt as 'one of the greatest royal ministers of all time',[2] Hubert Walter's achievement was to ensure that troops and money were sent across the Channel in quantities sufficient to win the approval of a demanding lord. Hubert's brother Theobald was put in charge of a unique 'state-run' tournament circuit whereby it was hoped to improve the fighting skills of English knights. Many years later William Marshal was to look back to the good old days of Richard's reign when 30 English knights were the equal of 40 French. English revenues as recorded in the Pipe Rolls averaged £25,000 a year over the five years 1194–98, but much more must have been raised. An important new revenue source – though one about which we have only scraps of information because, like all new sources, it was not subjected to the routine Exchequer audit – was opened up. This was a royal customs system introduced at the rate of one tenth on the value of overseas trade. Although we cannot estimate yield from this source, it is clear that the customs system allowed Richard to control seaborne trade sufficiently for the imposition of an embargo on trade with Flanders. In May 1194 Richard stayed at Portsmouth on his way back to Normandy. He granted the recently founded town its first royal charter and initiated the programme of investment on naval base and fleet of galleys that reflected both his own hands-on experience of naval and amphibious warfare in the Mediterranean and his determination to drive Philip out of the Channel. In 1196, according to Howden, Hubert told Richard that in the last two years he had sent him 1,100,000 marks – a fantastic total which must be either the chronicler's error or the minister's pardonable boast.

2 J. C. Holt, 'Ricardus rex Anglorum et dux Normannorum', in *Magna Carta and Medieval Government* (London, 1985).

Richard had no sooner returned to Normandy than one of Philip's allies deserted him. In May 1194 John killed the Capetian garrison of Evreux and handed the city back to Richard. According to William the Breton, he had first betrayed his father, then his brother and now our king. Once again the alliance with Navarre proved its worth. In 1194 a large force commanded by Berengaria's brother Sancho (later Sancho VII) laid the groundwork for the lightning campaign by which Richard restored his authority in the Touraine and Aquitaine, culminating in the capture of Angoulême itself (22 July 1194). As Ralph of Diceto observed with satisfaction, 'from the castle of Verneuil to the Cross of Charlemagne (in the Pyrenees) there was no one to stand up against him'. North of Verneuil, however, the task of recovery was to be very much more difficult. Philip was a shrewd politician and a competent soldier. He was well aware that eastern Normandy and the Seine valley were economically and strategically vital to the king of Paris. This was the region that had felt the main weight of his thrusts in 1193–94 and here he would fight tooth and nail to hold on to his conquests. When his sister Alice was returned to him in 1195 he at once married her to William of Ponthieu to reinforce his alliance with a lord whose county bordered Normandy. Even for a military commander as able and as renowned as Richard,[3] the task of recovery was bound to be difficult and expensive.

When the abbot of Crowland crossed the Channel to see Richard during a truce (August 1195), he found the king 'unable to attend to anything but campaigns, camps and castles'. Richard suffered setbacks, notably in the summer of 1196, but by 1198 the tide of war was flowing strongly in his favour. Norman revenues had been driven up to unprecedented levels (see p. 59). The Norman marcher lords had reverted to his allegiance. His diplomacy had won over Philip's former allies – even Toulouse. In October 1196 the new count of Toulouse, Raymond VI, married Richard's sister Joan; Richard restored the Quercy and gave them the county of Agen as Joan's dowry. In the summer of 1197 the new count of Flanders, Baldwin IX, was persuaded to change sides. For Baldwin alliance with Richard meant both an end to the embargo on trade with Flanders that Richard had imposed in 1194 and the hope of recovering Artois from Philip Augustus. In Germany the death of Emperor Henry VI was followed by a succession dispute; in July 1198 Baldwin attended the coronation

---

3  According to John France, *Western Warfare in the Age of the Crusades 1000–1300* (London, 1999), p. 142, he was 'undoubtedly the greatest commander within the period'.

at Aachen of Richard's candidate for the throne, his nephew Otto. Philip Augustus naturally supported Otto's rival, the Hohenstaufen candidate, Philip of Swabia, but this only had the effect of ensuring that the new pope, Innocent III, elected in January 1198, preferred Richard's man. Count Renaud of Boulogne, a celebrated warrior, also came into Richard's camp in 1198. According to William the Breton, not only Flanders and Boulogne, but also Count Louis of Blois and almost all the princes of the kingdom, some secretly, some openly, chose to desert their lawful king. There can be no doubt that Richard now outgunned Philip, forcing him to fight on at least two fronts at once. In 1197, for example, Count Baldwin outmanoeuvred Philip in Artois while Richard campaigned successfully in Berry. In 1198 Baldwin again invaded Artois, capturing Aire and St Omer, while Richard inflicted a humiliating defeat on the French king outside Gisors. Philip as well as Richard had been taxing hard, and he too was seen by his subjects as a financially oppressive ruler. By January 1199, when another truce was made, Richard held more territory in the Loire Valley than he had possessed in 1189 and in Normandy he had recovered nearly everything that had been lost. In the discussions that accompanied this truce Philip offered to restore everything except Gisors. But with the building of Les Andelys (see p. 73), Richard had constructed a fortified base from which he intended to carry out the reconquest of the whole Norman Vexin, Gisors included. To judge from the tone of Rigord of St Denis and William the Breton, and from the efforts they made to understand why God seemed to have abandoned Philip, morale at the Capetian court was low.

None the less Philip was not beaten. Naturally he hoped to pursue his old game of playing off one member of the Angevin dynasty against another. His new candidate for that role, Arthur of Brittany, born posthumously in 1187, had remained in his mother's care until 1196, when Richard tried to take charge of him. The Bretons resisted, found their duchy overrun by Richard's land and naval forces, but were able to get Arthur to safety at Philip's court. But as yet Arthur was still too young to be an active and effective instrument of Capetian policy. For the moment at least those perennially restless Aquitanian lords, the count of Angoulême and the viscount of Limoges, offered better hope. Encouraged by Philip they rebelled again and in March 1199 Richard went south to deal with them. At the siege of Chalus-Chabrol (near Limoges) he was struck by a crossbow bolt, and died on 6 April. God, wrote William the Breton, had come to save France.

# 5 The geography of the empire

It is easy enough to list the titles borne by Henry II and Richard I: king of the English, duke of the Normans and Aquitanians and count of the Angevins. By 1180, when Henry was at the height of his powers, he was also lord of Ireland and suzerain of Brittany and Toulouse. It is also possible to trace the borders of his dominions on a map. Sometimes this is easy. In places the border between Normandy and France was fairly well known; indeed, in 1169 Henry II ordered the construction of dykes to mark the line of the frontier. Elsewhere it is not so easy. Along the eastern border of Aquitaine, for example, we are dealing not with a clearly drawn line but with a frontier zone where Henry's and neighbouring princes' rights intermingled and overlapped. Particularly in these regions there was often a difference between the boundaries of the Angevin Empire as Henry *claimed* them to be and the boundaries as others saw them.

The map-maker's real problem comes when he decides how to show the area *within* the borders. A map of the Angevin Empire which implied – perhaps by shading all the provinces in a uniform colour – that their rule was equally effective everywhere would be seriously misleading. Less so, but none the less still misleading, would be a map on which the shading was varied so as to imply that some provinces, such as England, were intensively governed, while others, such as Aquitaine, were only lightly so. The chief drawback of such a map is that whereas England's political structure can fairly be represented by colouring the whole kingdom in one colour, with one or two clearly defined exceptions such as Durham and Cheshire, this cannot be said of any of the other Angevin dominions. By this date the kingdom of England had existed for more than 200 years; it had existed moreover with remarkably stable boundaries both externally, *vis-à-vis* other states, and internally, in the boundaries of the local administrative system of shire and hundred. England, it is true, had been conquered: by Cnut, by William I, by Henry II, but on each occasion it had been taken over intact, its regular institutions of government still in working order. Nowhere in the 'Celtic' and Gallic lands, not even in Normandy, was there anything to match this English administrative continuity. This contrast between England and the continental dominions is made explicit in a charter issued in favour of the Templars and confirmed by John in 1199. From each English shire which brought in £100 or more the Templars were to receive one mark; in Normandy, Maine, Anjou, Touraine, Poitou and Gascony they were to receive one mark, or its equivalent, from each city, castle or vill which rendered 100 pounds or more. In England, in other words, cities, castles and vills were enclosed within a uniform network of shires which, with a few exceptions, such as the Welsh march, covered the entire kingdom (Map 1). On the continent there was no such clear-cut pattern of local administration. In Anjou, for example, there were comital officials, sometimes *prévôts* (provosts), sometimes seneschals, sometimes both, based on the castles at Tours, Chinon, Baugé, Beaufort, Brissac, Angers, Saumur, Loudun, Loches, Langeais and Montbazon. They are to be found in the Loire Valley and in western Touraine; that is to say in those regions where the count held extensive demesne lands. Elsewhere in Anjou comital officials and comital castles are conspicuous by their absence. Here, and in Maine, we are in the land of the seigneurs. They recognized the count as their lord and might be expected to obey the count's representative, the seneschal of Anjou, but their own seigneurial organization was not overlain by a comital administrative unit equivalent to the shire. From their castles the barons of Anjou dominated the surrounding countryside, untroubled by the meddling of some local official who claimed to represent the count.

As Map 2 makes clear, there was a similar set-up in all the continental lands of the Angevins. In Gascony ducal officials were to be found only in Entre-deux-Mers, in the Bayonne-Dax region on the pilgrim road to Compostella and up the valley of the Garonne as far as Agen. Further north, in Poitou, the duke's castles were concentrated in Poitou proper. In the east of the province – in La Marche, the Limousin, Perigord and Angoumois – they were notably absent. In these regions indeed there were some lords who possessed some of the 'public' attributes of sovereign princes, the right to mint coins for example. There were non-ducal mints at Déols (until 1177),

**Map 1** Royal castles in England, Wales and Ireland

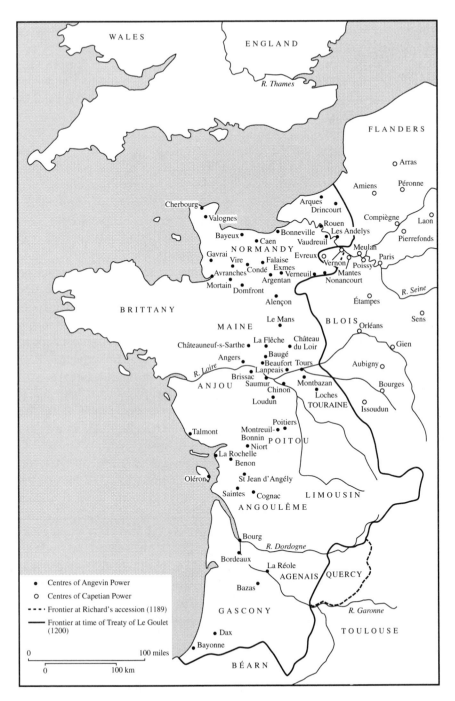

**Map 2** Angevin dominions on the continent, *c.* 1200

Turenne, Périgueux, Limoges and Angoulême – the only mints in the whole of the Angevin Empire (outside Brittany and Ulster) that were not under Plantagenet control. In Aquitaine, as in Anjou, it is not that ducal authority did not exist at all; it is rather that it was 'patchy'. This means that a political map of the Angevin Empire, if it is to be in any way meaningful, must be a map which takes account of that patchiness.

Of all the Angevin continental dominions Normandy was the least patchy. Indeed, one of the longterm consequences of the Norman Conquest of England had been the introduction of English administrative practice into the duchy. The local officials characteristic of eleventh-century Normandy – *prévôts* and *vicomtes* – found themselves increasingly, but by no means completely, eclipsed by a new type of executive and judicial (and therefore financial) official, the *bailli*. By 1200 there were about 25 *baillis* in the duchy at any one time and there was an observable tendency for their *bailliages* to become more shire-like, but as new creations of the twelfth century they were still subject to rearrangement and boundary alteration (as the English shire had been in the tenth century) according to immediate political or military need. This fact, plus the existence of great franchises like Eu, Aumale, Evreux and Alençon, meant that Normandy – as the privilege for the Templars indicates – still remained a land of cities and castellanies. Around 1200 ducal authority was relatively strong in the west of the duchy and along the frontiers (except on the north east) and relatively weak elsewhere (e.g. in the districts of Auge, Ouche and Caux).

One other point which needs to be borne in mind is that the patches could change in shape and size over time. In 1177 Henry II's great financial resources enabled him to acquire the county of La Marche (in eastern Poitou), to the chagrin of the Lusignan and Angoulême families who both thought they had a claim to succeed when the old count died leaving no direct heir. In Poitou as a whole there had been 10 ducal *prévôtés* in 1154; by 1189 there were 15. All five acquisitions (Talmont, Oléron, Cognac, Jarnac and Civray) were made after the war of 1173–74; they reflect Richard's emergence as an active and effective duke of Aquitaine. In Brittany Geoffrey was able to continue his father's work, bringing a number of local seneschals under the authority of an overall 'Seneschal of Brittany'. However, this was far from being an inexorable process of bureaucratization and the office seems to have lapsed when Constance married Ranulf of Chester.

Ireland, of course, was another country which was undergoing a drastic transformation, initially in the 1170s and then again after the appointment of John de Gray as justiciar in 1208. Yet despite the administrative development revealed in the Pipe Roll of 1212 and the flood of confiscations which marked John's expedition of 1210, the country as a whole remained essentially a land of seigneurs, whether they were Irish kings or English lords such as John de Courcy in Ulster. Wales, too, was a land of castles. Beyond Monmouth, Carmarthen was the only major castle of which the crown kept control throughout the reigns of Henry II and his sons. The rest of them were held either by Welsh princely dynasties or by English baronial houses. Both enjoyed what later constitutional lawyers would call 'sovereign' powers, notably the right to make war and peace. The feuds in which they engaged were only loosely and spasmodically supervised by the kings of England.

## CHARTERS, LAW COURTS AND JUSTICE

What were the practical day-to-day consequences of this contrast between England and the rest? Most English historians are inclined to regard England as the 'best governed' part. It is indeed possible to give some statistical support to this point of view. In the first two years of John's reign, for example, over 450 charters for English beneficiaries were enrolled (i.e. file copies were made for the royal archives) compared with less than 100 for both Normandy and Aquitaine and less than 50 for Anjou. It is clear from these figures that English property owners found it advantageous to seek royal charters and confirmations of charters. An analysis of Richard I's charters listed in the study of the king's itinerary by Lionel Landon showed that out of the 145 which were issued in Normandy no less than 91 were for English beneficiaries (compared with 49 for Normans, four for Angevins and one only for a Poitevin).[1] In the king's courts the king's charters provided the best possible proof of ownership, and from the reign of Henry II onwards the English royal administration was offering routine procedures for bringing cases to court. The flood of litigation which followed suggests that royal justice was relatively cheap, but whether it was more effective than

---

1 Figures for Richard's charters derived from an unpublished Cambridge MA dissertation by A. Cawley.

justice elsewhere is a question which is not easy to decide. Michael Clanchy has argued that in England 'the king's court raised expectations which it could not satisfy' and that 'ultimately everything depended on local opinion. In both civil and criminal cases the essential decisions were made by the verdicts of jurors from the neighbourhood and not by the judges from Westminster.'[2] But in that case it is not easy to see why 'local opinion' in England should be more effective than a similar commodity in Poitou. Did an English property-owner really sleep more easily in his bed than his Poitevin equivalent? Or did he curse the fact that in order for him to manipulate English local opinion in the way he wanted, it was sometimes necessary for him to go on long and expensive journeys – by sea as well as by land – in search of the itinerant royal court? Poitevins, it may be, found the customs of dispute settlement in Poitou at least as manageable.

Not indeed that they were always so different in England. Private war was, it is true, prohibited in England – as it also was in Normandy – whereas in Poitou the feud was a traditional part of the legal system. But in reality it was not always quite as simple as this. In 1201, for example, a dispute between Abbot Samson of Bury St Edmunds and Bishop Eustace of Ely (both of them veritable pillars of the establishment) was taken to court and decided in Bury's favour by reference to the terms of a royal charter; not, indeed, by reference to the actual charter in the hands of the beneficiary – for charters, as was only too well known, could be forged, but by reference to the copy found in the charter rolls. What could be more rational and peaceful than this? Unfortunately the court's verdict still had to be enforced. When a steward of the abbot of Bury read out the king's letter he was 'treated with great abuse and violence', so Abbot Samson ordered a night raid by 600 well-armed men. They carried off all their adversary's cattle and did what damage they could. In other words they prosecuted a feud: the intention was to 'persuade' local opinion that the verdict of the king's court should stand. In this case we have to turn to chronicle evidence (the famous Bury Chronicle of Jocelin of Brakelond) in order to see what was really going on behind the formal record of court proceedings. Historians of Henry II's 'legal reforms' or of John's supposed devotion to the business of justice tend to approach the judicial evidence in an optimistic frame of mind, to see England as a peaceful and

2  M. T. Clanchy, *England and its Rulers, 1066–1272* (2nd edn., Oxford 1998), p. 109.

well-governed land. But a more pessimistic view is possible. To Maitland it seemed that in England John's reign was 'a holiday for murderers and robbers'.[3] By contrast with the other parts of the Angevin Empire, England was administered in a remarkably uniform and centralized fashion by a government which kept a systematic record of its activities. Whether it was the 'best' governed part is another matter.

## ENGLISH ROYAL REVENUES 1130–1220

At the most material level England might be said to have been – from the ruler's point of view – the best-governed part if it could be shown that it was, in financial terms, the most productive part. Sometimes it is taken for granted that it was. Frequently a patriotic note can be heard when English historians write of the English tax-payer being bled white to pay for Plantagenet wars across the Channel – less respectable activities than wars against Welsh or Scots which at least had 'the virtue' of tending towards the creation of Great Britain. 'England', we are told, had to pay for Richard I's crusade; 'England' had to raise the king's ransom. It is true that if we look at English records we get an impression of large quantities of 'English' silver being shipped overseas. The roads between London, Winchester and Southampton or Portsmouth, then the sea lanes to Rouen or Caen, have been graphically described as 'a treasure route, as essential to the fortunes of the Angevin house as the bullion fleets from America were to the cause of the Hapsburg kings of Spain in the sixteenth and seventeenth centuries'.[4] Does this mean that England was 'the milch cow of the Angevin Empire' and that the continental dominions were poor, too poor to pay their own way?

The problem here is that England is the only part of the Angevin Empire for which we can compile a series of figures for the king's minimum annual revenue. Exchequer accounting documents, the pipe rolls, survive in a virtually unbroken series beginning with the second financial year of Henry II's reign (1156 or, more precisely, Michaelmas 1155 to Michaelmas 1156). Interpreting the pipe rolls is

3 F. W. Maitland (ed.) *Select Pleas of the Crown, i, 1200–1225* (London, 1888), p. xxiv.
4 J. C. Holt, 'Ricardus rex Anglorum et dux Normannorum', in *Riccardo Cuor di Leone nella Storia e nella Leggenda*, Academia Nazionale dei Lincei: problemi attuali di scienza e di cultura, 253 (1981), p. 29, reprinted in *Magna Carta and Medieval Government* (London, 1985).

a complicated business (see pp. 69–70); in general, they were records of audits of routine sources of revenue and take no account of extra-ordinary or newly introduced sources of income. In some years exceptional measures, for example, the Saladin Tithe of 1188 or the taxes levied in 1193–94 to pay Richard's ransom, brought in massive additional sums (though not only in England). A tax in 1207, the Thirteenth, is recorded as having yielded £57,421, and the Fifteenth of 1225 produced about £40,000, but except in these two thirteenth-century cases we can do no more than hazard guesses at what was raised by such special measures.

What the long series of pipe rolls does show very clearly, however, is that political vicissitudes had a dramatic effect on royal revenue – defining revenue as treasury receipts (i.e. cash received) plus autho-rized expenditure. Thus revenue at the start of Henry II's reign, aver-aging about £10,500 a year during the three years 1156–58, was less than half that indicated by the one surviving pipe roll of Henry I's reign. According to this roll Henry I's revenue in 1130 was of the order of £23,500. Evidently the troubled days of King Stephen's reign had cost the crown dear. Then the recovery of royal authority in England meant that by the last ten years of Henry II's reign recorded English revenue averaged almost £22,000 a year. Crusade preparations led to an 1190 pipe roll total of £31,089, followed by a steep drop to only £11,000 a year while Richard I was on crusade. When Richard returned to his dominions – and had to fight a costly war – recorded revenue climbed to average £25,000 over the five years 1194–98. John's pipe roll revenue fluctuated between £22,000 and £25,000 for 1199–1203, and then rose steeply reaching over £50,000 in 1210 and 1212, with an astonishing high-point of £83,291 in 1211. (Indeed, as a result of interdict profits and tallages on Jews – revenues not subjected to routine exchequer audit – John's income from England in 1210–12 was certainly even higher, possibly reaching a staggering £145,000 in 1211.) No roll survives for 1213, but the political difficulties which John faced at the end of his reign are reflected in the totals of £25,712 for 1214 and £18,463 for 1215. For the first three years of Henry III's reign for which pipe rolls survive, 1218–20, revenue averages only £8,000 – an astonishingly low figure, less even than the equivalent totals for the 1150s, despite the fact that inflation had led, roughly, to a doubling of prices between 1130 and 1220. Given the overwhelming weight of indirect evidence for the demographic, economic and commercial expansion of the period between 1150 and 1220, what emerges beyond all doubt is that fluctuations in royal revenue reflected political fortunes far more closely than they did economic trends. The fiscal consequences of Stephen's reign, of Richard's crusade, of John's oppressive government after 1207, of the reaction to it in 1214 and 1215, and of the politically fragile post-civil war situation of Henry III's minority, are all very apparent

## OTHER REVENUES

### Ireland

By contrast with the impressive run of pipe roll figures from England, the financial records of all the other Angevin dominions are either non-existent or less than adequate. The evidence of the Irish pipe roll of 1212 – the only one to survive from this period of Irish history – can be combined with the record of treasure sent to England in John's reign to indicate that the lordship of Ireland could provide the king with about £2,000 a year.

### Normandy

Three more or less complete Norman exchequer rolls survive: for 1180, 1195 and 1198. In 1180 Norman revenue was about 27,000 *livres angevins* (£6,750), less than half the amount – £14,300 – that was raised in England that year. In 1195 yield was over 80,000 *l.a.* This sum includes a substantial contribution to Richard's ransom; deducting that still left the duke with about 51,000 *l.a.* (£12,750). By 1198 Norman revenue had risen to 99,000 *l.a.* (nearly £25,000) – not far short of four times as much as in 1180. This increase, in part a consequence of exploiting new revenue sources, in part no doubt a reflection of the near-permanent presence of the king himself in Normandy, has been dubbed the 'Norman fiscal revolution'.[5] That nearly £25,000 should have been raised in Normandy in 1198 is all the more remarkable in view of the likelihood that the population of Normandy was considerably smaller than that of England. Every three years the duke had the right to take a tax, the *fouage*, assessed on each hearth in the duchy. According to the earliest record of the

5 V. Moss, 'The Norman fiscal revolution, 1193–98', in W. M. Ormrod, M. Bonney and R. Bonney (eds), *Crises, Revolutions and Self Sustained Growth: Essays in European Fiscal History 1130–1830* (Stamford, 1999).

income from *fouage,* in 1221 it brought in 15,384 livres 9s. 0d.; at the rate of 12d. per hearth this would mean 307,689 hearths and, using a multiplier of five people per hearth, this suggests a Norman population in that year of over one and a half million. Obviously this is a very rough and ready sort of calculation but it suggests that an estimate of 1,500,000 for the population of Normandy *c.* 1200 may not be too wide of the mark. We can only guess at the population of England at that time but since estimates of the Domesday (1086) population vary between 1,250,000 and 2,250,000 and all agree that the twelfth century witnessed demographic growth (though at an unknown rate), it seems highly likely that it was greater, and possibly considerably greater, than that of Normandy. A recent informed guess puts the English population *c.*1200 at 3.5 to 4 million.[6] All this suggests that if in 1130 England was relatively heavily taxed – the most likely explanation for this being the tenurial and fiscal consequence of 1066 – and that as late as 1180 Normandy was still relatively lightly taxed, none the less by the late 1190s the duchy was at least paying its share, and may even have been more of a milch cow than England. What we know of the financial contribution of towns to the ruler's purse points in the same direction. In 1198, for example, both Caen and Rouen had to find more money than did London.

## Anjou and Aquitaine

The hardest problem of all is to estimate the revenues of Anjou and Aquitaine. No financial accounts survive from the Angevin period but it does not follow from this that the revenues were insignificant. They are unknown and we must make a judgement as to whether we think them large or small. On the basis of a 1221 account for Anjou and a 1238 account for Poitou, historians have generally been inclined to think that they were small. But the early thirteenth-century political vicissitudes in Anjou and Poitou (see below pp. 97–8, 105) mean that this is rather like estimating Henry II's and Richard's income on the basis of figures derived from the early pipe rolls of Henry III's reign. Against this a glance at the map would appear to suggest that the revenues were considerable. The area contains some very fertile regions, notably the valleys of the Loire,

---

6  J. L. Bolton, 'The English economy in the early thirteenth century', in S. D. Church (ed.), *King John: New Interpretations* (Woodbridge, 1999) p. 32.

the Charente and the Garonne. In the Loire Valley were the vineyards of Anjou and Touraine and the great town of Tours, famous
for its fine metalwork. As for the economy of Aquitaine, the learned
English chronicler Ralph of Diceto described it in glowing terms:

> Aquitaine overflows with riches of many kinds, excelling other parts of
> the western world to such an extent that historians consider it to be one
> of the most fortunate and flourishing of the provinces of Gaul. Its fields
> are fertile, its vineyards productive and its forests teem with wild life.
> From the Pyrenees northwards the whole countryside is irrigated by the
> River Garonne and other streams, indeed it is from these lifegiving
> waters [aquae] that the province takes its name.[7]

Obviously this wealth did not go entirely untapped. In addition to
demesne revenues, the *prévôts* of Anjou and Aquitaine were
expected to collect profits of justice, tallages and other local dues,
often known comprehensively as 'exactions'. The revenues of
Chinon included a *commune*. In the south this term was sometimes
used to describe a peace-tax, such as that which Richard imposed on
the Bordelais in 1195–96. This was a levy assessed partly on live-
stock and partly on a valuation of movable property. The peace was
to last for ten years and presumably the tax was to be collected each
year. By 1204 a new ruler, Philip Augustus, was working on the
assumption that the seneschals of Poitou and Anjou might be asked
to impose and account for taxes on both Christians and Jews and
that they were entitled to an annual payment of 50 *livres* and a mark
of silver from each *prévôté* within their jurisdiction. Fragmentary
evidence of this kind does not allow us to make any sort of guess at
the revenues of Anjou and Aquitaine but it does at least point to the
existence of a functioning financial administration. There was clearly
an important treasury at Chinon. When Richard defied his father in
1187 he at once seized Chinon. In 1199 when John heard the news
of his brother's death his first thought was to dash to Chinon.

## THE ANGEVIN TRADING ZONE

It is also worth considering the part which Anjou and Aquitaine
played in a wider economic context. Economically speaking, the
Angevin Empire may be described as a number of complementary

---

7 *Radulfi de Diceto Opera Historica*, W. Stubbs (ed.), 2 vols (London, 1876), vol. 1, pp.
293–4.

regions bound together by a series of well-defined waterways. As producers and exporters of salt and wine Anjou and Aquitaine made a major contribution to the commercial prosperity of the empire as a whole. Salt, one of the indispensable ingredients of medieval life, was produced along almost the whole length of the Atlantic coast of France. The main varieties were 'Bay Salt' from the Bay of Bourgneuf in the marches between Poitou and Brittany, the salt of Brouage, panned on the sheltered shores behind the isles of Oléron and Ré, and, in the far south, the salt of Bayonne. For the twelfth century, however, we are much better informed about the rapidly expanding wine trade. The best wines of Anjou and Touraine – the *vins pour la mer* – were taken down to the sea via Nantes. There is plenty of evidence for the planting of new vineyards in the Bordelais and even a patriotic Poitevin was prepared to admit that Bordeaux wine was of superb quality. But at this date by far the most important wine-exporting region was in Poitou itself, in Aunis and Saintonge. A fine white wine was produced around Niort, St Jean d'Angély and La Rochelle and then shipped overseas from Niort and, above all, from La Rochelle. Another product exported in increasing quantities via La Rochelle from the late twelfth century onwards was the fine quality pottery produced in kilns around La Chapelle-des-Pots (near Saintes) and known to archaeologists as Saintonge ware.

La Rochelle was a new town, possibly the most successful new town in the whole of twelfth-century Europe. Founded in 1130 it very quickly came to enjoy all the characteristics of a boom town, looked upon by its rivals as a sink of iniquity where the *nouveaux riches* wallowed in the luxury obtained from trade. Its modern quays were well suited to accommodate the new large ships, known as cogs, which in the course of the second half of the twelfth century came to dominate the maritime trade of the Baltic, North Sea, Channel and Atlantic coasts. Using these ships the merchants of La Rochelle could compete in the markets of England, Normandy and Flanders with wines produced nearer at hand, in the Paris Basin, the Rhineland and in England too. La Rochelle's wealth meant that it attracted Jews and Templars and became an important financial and banking centre. It is no accident that international maritime law came to be based on a custom known as the Laws of Oléron.

The importance of the wine trade can be judged from the fact that one of John's first acts as king of England was to issue an assize of wines, fixing the prices at which the wines of Poitou and Anjou were to be sold. Perhaps the measure was intended to boost the popularity of the new ruler. The prices were set rather low and as a result, commented Roger of Howden, 'the whole land was filled with drink and drinkers'. Not everyone gained. English winegrowers, for example, cannot have been overjoyed to see themselves put out of business by the competition from Anjou and Poitou. But then, as one late-twelfth-century writer put it, English wine could be drunk only with closed eyes and through clenched teeth, so presumably the consumer was happy with the exchange. The increasing volume of products from western France, in other words, was being fed into a system of commodity exchange which included hides from Ireland, grain, tin and cloth from England, building stone, woad and grain from Normandy. There is no more dramatic illustration of the importance of this sea-borne commerce than the early thirteenth-century (and still functioning) lighthouse at Hook near Waterford in Ireland, among medieval monuments a unique survival.

There can be no doubt that this growing commerce was a source of great profit to the Angevins. As lords of many of the major ports of north-western Europe – Bayonne, Bordeaux, La Rochelle, Nantes, Rouen, Dublin, Bristol, Southampton and London – they ruled over an immense trading zone. It was a trading zone with, as the archaeological record shows, a very long pre-history, and one which, as coin hoards show, was now becoming increasingly a 'sterling zone'. Since in many cases they ruled over consumers as well as producers, ports of import as well as ports of export, they were beautifully placed to impose tolls and customs duties. Once again the English exchequer records provide the kind of information which is available from no other part of the empire. They demonstrate that by 1194–95 Richard I had introduced a customs duty levied at the rate of one-tenth. In that year William of Yarmouth accounted for £537 14s 2d from the tenth raised in the ports of Norfolk and Lincolnshire, but because as with other revenues raised from new sources, customs revenue was not systematically subjected to the bureaucratic procedure of an exchequer audit, the national yield is unknown. The pipe roll for 1203–4 reveals that nearly £5,000 was collected from the ports of the south and east coasts from Fowey to Newcastle in the sixteen months between July 1203 and November 1204.

On the other hand, the innumerable letters of protection, safe-conduct and exemption from paying 'our customs' which are enrolled on the chancery rolls cover the whole empire and from them, though we can compile no statistics, we can get a better impression of the scale of the system. Several things stand out. One is the importance of three rivers – the Seine, the Loire and the Garonne – and of three commodities: grain, salt going upstream and wine coming downstream. Another is the ruler's propensity to levy more or higher customs duties. In 1199, for example, Eleanor freed the citizens of Bordeaux from various 'evil, unheard of and unlawful customs'. The usual term for such customs – presumably 'unlawful' because either new or set at a higher than customary rate – was 'maltote'. Chapter 41 of Magna Carta abolished maltotes in England; and there were maltotes on the Continent too. In 1202 John ordered merchants carrying wine and salt on the Seine to pay 'the maltote which they had been accustomed to pay in the time of Richard our brother'. In 1216 he ordered that his debt to some wine merchants should be repaid out of the customs and maltotes on wine at Bordeaux and La Réole. A third point to note is that although La Rochelle figures quite largely in the rolls – as an entrepôt in the horse trade, for example – there are very few references to customs duties there. This suggests that the rulers were careful about granting exemptions on wine exports from there. At any rate it is clear that the revenues generated at La Rochelle were very considerable. In 1199 John was prepared to pay a high price in order to buy out the residual rights which the Mauléon family claimed to hold there.

Although the Angevins imposed tolls, and granted – doubtless at a price – licences to other lords to do the same, they presumably offered the merchants something in return. One of the most striking facts about Angevin political history is the consistent loyalty of the towns. In the Norman crisis of 1203–4 the towns were prepared to resist Philip when many were not. In 1205–6 Alfonso of Castile was halted at the gates of Bordeaux and Bayonne. By 1220 urban authorities in Aquitaine were desperate to maintain their links with the government in England. The mayor and commune of Niort wrote to Henry III:

> on bended knee and with tears in our eyes we implore and beseech you in every way we can to send us a governor who will defend both us and your land of Poitou. . . . Do not appoint someone from around here as seneschal, but send us a noble, prudent and influential man from England.

Moreover, towns such as La Rochelle, Niort and Bordeaux were prepared to back up their begging letters with money of their own. Only their loans prevented the complete collapse of ducal administration in Aquitaine during the impoverished minority of Henry III.

In 1173–74 when many Poitevins had followed Eleanor and Richard into revolt against Henry II, La Rochelle had stood out for its loyalty to the Old King; and in the end it was the fall of La Rochelle, in 1224, which marked the real end of the Angevin Empire. So too it was the loyalty of Bordeaux and Bayonne in 1224 (as in 1205–6) that kept Hugh of Lusignan at bay, and so ensured the survival of English Gascony.

How are we to explain this consistent loyalty? In part no doubt by the fact that the Angevins were sometimes prepared to give the towns what they wanted, in particular the degree of self-government which was guaranteed by communal status. By 1204 no fewer than 17 Norman towns had been granted communes; and outside Normandy by the same date there were communes at La Rochelle, Bayonne, Dax, Oléron, Niort, St-Jean d'Angély, Saintes and St-Émilion. The most famous urban privilege of Normandy, the *Établissements de Rouen*, was enjoyed by non-Norman as well as by Norman towns. But in most cases the grant of a commune is likely to have been the reward for a pre-existing loyalty – as it certainly was at La Rochelle after 1173–74 and at Bordeaux after 1205–6 – so its purpose was to reinforce rather than create. Presumably what really counted was that the urban ruling elites believed that the Angevin Empire was in some sense 'good for business' and should, therefore, be supported. They were very likely right. While, for example, England and Poitou were ruled by one and the same prince it was reasonable to expect that trade between England and Poitou would be permitted, perhaps even protected and encouraged. Ruled by different princes there was always the possibility of war between them and the ports of one being closed to the other.

When Philip conquered Normandy he refused to permit ships carrying wine from Poitou, Gascony and Anjou to enter the duchy. This prohibition must have dismayed all the merchants involved and although it was probably lifted in 1206 – when John and Philip agreed to a truce – it is clear that the conquest of Normandy was a serious blow to the prosperity of Rouen (now less favourably treated than its up-river rival, Paris) as well as to cross-Channel ports like Dieppe and Barfleur. Similarly, Louis VIII's conquest of Poitou had a damaging effect on the trade of La Rochelle. In future it would be the wine merchants of Bordeaux, not those of La Rochelle, who made themselves rich on the English connection. In these circumstances it is hardly surprising that merchants were opposed to the break-up of the Angevin Empire. In their eyes it was a unified governmental structure which offered the benefits of relative political stability to an immense trading area.

The Angevin Empire was held together not merely by genealogical accident but also by the mutual interest of a number of complementary – and increasingly interdependent – economies. Given the economic advantages enjoyed by water transport, this means that sea-lanes and rivers were the backbone of the empire. In particular the sea-route hugging the western and north-western coasts of France was a vital life-line. Consider the state of the continental dominions in 1205: at this critical moment John ruled little more than Bayonne, Bordeaux, La Rochelle, Oléron and the Channel Islands – a string of ports and the sea-lane which connected them with Britain. Yet on this seemingly narrow base John was able to rally and stage a partial recovery. That the government was well aware of the importance of this route is shown by the strenuous efforts they made to recover and retain control of important points along it: the Channel Islands (recovered in 1205 and even today kept out of the hands of the successors of the Capetians); the isle of Oléron (lost in 1224, recovered in 1230 and held until 1294). The Angevin Empire, in other words, was not just a bundle of territories, it was also a sea-borne empire. When Richard went on crusade he took the sea route. So too, of course, did Philip Augustus but whereas the king of France hired a fleet from Genoa, Richard assembled a great fleet from his own dominions and no less than four out of the five fleet commanders were men from western France. Seen in this light Anjou and Aquitaine were not mere appendages which cost the English taxpayer dear. They were regions which made an important economic and financial contribution to the empire as a whole. Without them it would have been distinctly poorer.

# 6 Government

John Le Patourel described Angevin government as 'a three-tiered structure'.[1] At the top, the king and the royal household. In the middle, the administrations of the provinces of the empire – Anjou, Normandy, Poitou, Gascony, England, Brittany and Ireland, each of them organized and directed by a seneschal (in the continental territories) or by a justiciar (in England and Ireland). At the bottom, the administrations of local officials: sheriffs, reeves, *baillis, vicomtes* and *prévôts*. Local administration is discussed elsewhere (pp. 51–4). Here I begin at the top.

## KING AND HOUSEHOLD

The most important component of Angevin government was the king himself. His personal character still counted for more than any other single factor – as is obvious from the contrast between the reigns of Richard and John.

Naturally the king could not govern alone. Wherever he went he was followed by a great crowd: courtiers, officials, servants, traders, petitioners and hangers-on of every description. The late twelfth-century writer Walter Map has left a memorable picture of Henry II in the thick of the throng. 'Whenever he goes out he is seized by the crowd and pulled and pushed hither and thither; he is assaulted by shouts and roughly handled; yet he listens to all with patience and seemingly without anger; until hustled beyond bearing he silently retreats to some place of quiet.'[2] The king was both a cult figure and a ruler. His court was always a centre of culture, of fashion and of scandal. Henry de la Mare held three estates in return for

---

1 J. Le Patourel, 'The Plantagenet dominions', *History* 50 (1965), p. 298.
2 Walter Map, *De Nugis Curialium: Courtier's Trifles*, ed. and trans. M. R. James, reissued by C. N. L. Brooke and R. A. B. Mynors (Oxford, 1983).

service at court: one for guarding the door of the king's hall and two for supervising the prostitutes.

At the centre of the crowd that followed him was the king's household. In part, this was an elaborate domestic service: cooks, butlers, larderers, grooms, tentkeepers, carters, sumpter men and the bearer of the king's bed. There were also the men who looked after his hunt, the keepers of the hounds, the horn-blowers, the archers. Then there were the men whose work was political, military and administrative as well as domestic. Some of them had fairly well-defined functions. The chancellor was responsible for the king's seal and the chancery clerks. Treasurer and chamberlains looked after the king's money and valuables. Constables and marshals were in charge of military organization; they had the job of mobilizing the household knights and of ensuring that they were paid their annual fees and then wages reckoned according to the number of days they served. But the household, like the king, was omnicompetent and a member of the household was likely to find himself entrusted with a wide variety of political and military tasks. In the autumn of 1159, for example, it was the chancellor, Thomas Becket, who was left in charge of military operations against the count of Toulouse. Here, in the household, lay both the mainspring of government and the core of the king's army.

Some of these household officials were clerks. In this period the chancellor and the treasurer always were. But many of them were laymen: the chamberlains, the stewards, the constables, the marshals – and also, of course, the household knights. Not only did these kings *not* depend exclusively, or even primarily, upon clerks for the administrative skills necessary to rule a country, they also did *not* rely on a group of royal officials whose interests were pitted against the interests of the great landholders, the magnates. On the contrary the king's household normally included some of the most powerful barons. Servants in the king's household, they were also lords of great estates and therefore masters of their own households. Through their influence the authority of the crown was carried into the localities. This informal power system was often reinforced by the appointment of members of the household to provincial or local office. In Walter Map's phrase, an able king governed his dominions 'like a good *pater-familias* ruling a single household'.[3]

3  Walter Map. *Courtiers' Trifles*, p. 485.

# CENTRAL ADMINISTRATION

The two main household offices were the chamber and the chancery, but it is worth noting that, although we undoubtedly can differentiate between one department and the other, the clerical staff who manned them were simply the king's clerks and might serve in either.

## Chamber

The chamber was the financial office of the itinerant household and, as such, the government's chief spending department. It poured out money in great quantities, particularly on warfare and the king's sport. Where did this money come from? Some, in the form of silver pennies barrelled or in sacks of £100 each, was transferred to it from the main treasuries (attached to the exchequers) at London and Caen. Some came from the treasures stored in royal castles. During Henry II's reign there were castle treasuries in England at Gloucester, Colchester, Salisbury, Oxford and Guildford; in Normandy at Rouen, Falaise and Argentan. Further south we run into the usual problem of lack of evidence but it is at least clear that there was an extremely important castle treasury at Chinon, and likely that similar ones existed at Loches, Poitiers and Bordeaux. Then there were additional sums which were paid directly into the chamber, for example, some payments made by the king's debtors. When these payments involved sums which were normally accounted for at the exchequer, then the exchequer had to be notified, but of other chamber receipts – for example, loans to the king – there may be no record. This is why the financial records of the court of the exchequer, the pipe rolls, provide only an incomplete statement of monies received (see also p. 58). They are useful as a general guide to royal resources but they do not allow us to measure income with a high degree of accuracy.

It was the chamber that was the central and controlling organ of the royal financial system; wherever the king went, his chamber clerks and their carts loaded with silver pennies and chamber records went with him. Chamberlains like Hubert de Burgh and clerks of the chamber like Philip of Poitiers and Walter of Coutances ended their careers holding the highest offices.

Compared with the chamber, the exchequers of England and Normandy were merely useful auxiliaries. Unfortunately, the extant documentation tends to give precisely the opposite impression. The only twelfth-century records to survive in any quantity are exchequer records not chamber records. It is clear that chamber records were kept, perhaps from as early as the eleventh century, but the earliest surviving chamber rolls date from John's reign. Only with the proliferation of records in the thirteenth century does the central importance of the chamber emerge from obscurity. Before that date only those revenues that touched upon the exchequer system can be counted and in consequence historians sometimes write as though it were only exchequer revenues that counted: in geographical terms as though it were only the English and Norman revenues that counted, i.e. were large enough to be worth counting. But clearly if powerful kings were capable of paying for their activities without using an exchequer – and the history of all pre-twelfth-century kings and princes throughout Europe suggests that they were – this would be a very dangerous conclusion.

*Chancery*

The chancery was the secretarial department of the household. Not surprisingly it is in this department that the proliferation of government records which characterizes the whole period takes its most dramatic form. Chancery clerks had long been responsible for drawing up royal charters and writs. In the 1170s they also began to keep records of promises of payment to the king in return for grants of land or other favours (these promises are known, somewhat confusingly, as fines); at intervals extracts from these records were sent to the exchequer. These extracts were 'enrolled', i.e. copied on to parchment sheets sewn together end to end and then rolled up: they are known as fine rolls. During the period of Hubert Walter's chancellorship (1199–1205) the proliferation of records reached explosive proportions. From then on registers in the form of rolls were kept of nearly all outgoing letters. For the historian of government the advent of the chancery rolls means an abrupt transition: from a period when he is struggling to do the best he can with too little evidence to a period when he has almost too much and he has to work hard not to be submerged under a flood of documents.

The period of rapid bureaucratic development under Hubert Walter's orderly management coincides – and it seems to be no more than a coincidence – with the political and military crisis of the Angevin Empire: the loss of Anjou, Normandy and much of Poitou. For the historian interested in questions of the empire's administrative coherence this is a coincidence which creates formidable problems of interpretation.

Some chancery records, in particular the most famous of them, the charter rolls (begun in the first year of John's reign) and the patent rolls (begun in his third year), deal with government business from every province and show that for some administrative purposes the Angevin Empire could be treated as a single whole. Other chancery records suggest that in other administrative contexts it was found more convenient to divide the empire, not, however, into half a dozen separate provinces but into two parts: one insular, the other continental. From 1199 onwards two sets of fine rolls were kept: one roll recording debts which were to be collected by the Norman exchequer, the other recording those which concerned the English exchequer. Whereas a run of English fine rolls survives to this day, only one Norman roll (from the second year of John's reign, 1200–1) is still extant. Significantly, it contains not only Norman material but also a few entries relating to Anjou and Poitou. The earliest Close Rolls follow a similar pattern. Beginning in 1200–1 we find the chancery making enrolments of writs authorizing payments by the exchequer. Here also two sets of rolls were kept, one for England and Ireland and the other for the king's continental dominions. Although the latter are conventionally known as 'Norman rolls' they in fact contain a good deal of business from Aquitaine and Anjou. In the roll of 1200–1, for example, writs sent to William des Roches, the seneschal of Anjou, were sufficiently common for the copying clerk to write his name by mistake. The practice of lumping all the continental lands together and treating them as an administrative unit may well reflect a habit of mind which looked upon the Channel as though it were the Alps; thinking of lands as being either across the Channel or on this side of it. Thus Roger of Howden, an English chronicler who was also a royal clerk, could refer to the continental dominions *en bloc* as *totam terram transmarinam*.

In the event, this two-part administrative structure lasted only until the spring of 1203. King Philip's conquest of Anjou tore the heart out of John's inheritance. It had the effect of snapping all routine administrative links between Normandy and the other continental lands. From then on the 'Norman rolls' contain nothing but Norman business – until the duchy too succumbed little more than a year later. In May 1204, when John conceded defeat, the Norman archives were sent from Caen to Shoreham and thence in carts to London. By a nice irony of history those voluminous records which make it possible, for the first time, to uncover the administrative structure of the Angevin Empire, reveal – at the same time – the way in which that structure was undermined by the political and military crisis of John's reign.

One further, apparently minor, administrative detail deserves to be emphasized. The chancery made two copies of each fine roll. One copy was sent to the appropriate exchequer; the other was retained in the chancery. Surviving chancery copies contain notes totalling the amount of money the king was owed from this source. Since such totals would obviously have been useful to anyone trying to estimate future income it is significant that it is the chancery copies, not the exchequer ones, which are annotated in this way. It is further proof, if any were needed, that central control over the financial system rested with the household, not with the exchequer.

## THE ITINERANT HOUSEHOLD

Clearly it was in the king's political interest to have a large and impressive court and in the interests of ambitious men to become members. None the less, the household could not simply grow *ad infinitum*; transport and catering problems were alone sufficient to see to that. The demands made by the household had a dramatic effect on local foodstocks and prices and created a situation wide open to abuse. The presence of the king imposed a heavy burden on any district through which he passed; only one or two particularly prosperous regions could endure him and his household for any length of time. So the king was constantly on the move. He travelled both for political reasons (in order to make his presence felt) and for economic reasons (to make his presence no longer felt). The sheer size of their dominions meant that in this respect the Angevin kings had to work very hard – though Henry II's own courtiers explained the king's incessant movement in terms of his fear of getting fat. At times the wagons of the household averaged twenty miles a day – and they went on moving, winter and summer. A system of household government meant, as Jolliffe put it, 'a government of the roads and roadsides'.[4]

But which roads? An answer to this question might give us a clue to Angevin territorial and political priorities. Unfortunately it is only

4 J. E. A. Jolliffe, *Angevin Kingship* (2nd edn, London, 1963), p. 140.

from 1199 that we can trace the king's itinerary on something approaching a day-to-day basis. Fortunately, however, this means that there are at least a few years (1199–1202) in which we can follow the movements of a king who was still ruler of the whole Angevin Empire. From the beginning of his reign in April 1199 to the end of 1202 John spent roughly 45 per cent of his time in Normandy, 25 per cent in England, 22 per cent in Greater Anjou and 8 per cent in Aquitaine (*see* Map 3). Although the evidence for his predecessors' itineraries is much less good, it seems likely that the basic pattern was a similar one. As Robert Bartlett has observed:'Any of the Norman and Angevin kings who were able to do so spent more time in France than in England. The only kings of England to spend prolonged periods in England were the military failures.'[5]

Le Patourel's rough calculation for Henry II was that he spent 176 months in Normandy, 154 in England, Wales and Ireland and 84 in the French lands other than Normandy.[6] In the last five years of his reign, after his return from crusade and imprisonment, Richard spent slightly more than three years in Normandy, one in Anjou, eight months in Aquitaine and less than two months in England.

What these calculations suggest is that Normandy was central for all three Angevin kings and that it was even more important from the 1190s onwards. In view of Normandy's geographical position, offering sea approaches to England as well as sea and land routes to the other continental dominions, and in view of the increasing military pressure exerted by Philip Augustus, both the basic pattern and its intensification in the 1190s can be readily explained. What is worth noting though is that, so far as his itinerary is concerned, John, who in 1203 spent almost the whole year in Normandy, was a typical Angevin ruler. For as long as he could, he spent most of his time on the Continent. He became an English king only by default and against his will.

There was, it is often said, 'no capital but the king's highway'. In a strict sense this is true but what the map of John's itinerary in the years 1199 to 1202 shows is that there was something approaching a capital on the 20-mile highway between Rouen and Les Andelys (the palace, river-port and towns which lay at the foot of Richard I's great Castle of the Rock, Château-Gaillard). Out of the five places which John visited most frequently no less than four – in ranking

5 R. Bartlett, *England under the Norman and Angevin Kings 1075–1225* (Oxford, 2000), p. 13.
6 Le Patourel, 'The Plantagenet dominions', op. cit., p. 295 n. 14.

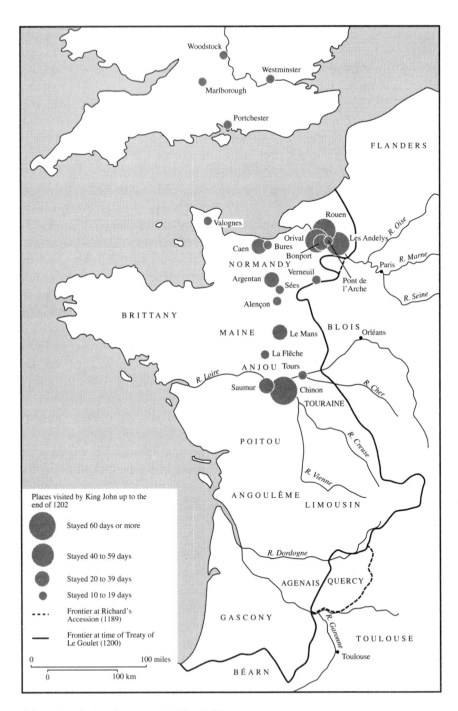

**Map 3** John's itinerary, 1199–1202

order Rouen, Les Andelys, Orival and Bonport – were located in this small stretch of the Seine Valley. This core area was very largely Richard's creation. He built Château-Gaillard and Les Andelys; he founded the Cistercian abbey at Bonport; he spent further sums on bridges, castles and royal residences at Pont de l'Arche, Portjoie, Orival, Radepont, Vaudreuil, Boutavant and Cléry. The fact that Richard built a fleet of galleys (no less than 70 of them, according to William the Breton) is a further striking indication of his determination to control both the River Seine and the Channel crossing.

Much less developed than the Rouen–Les Andelys capital region but possessing some of the same characteristics was the stretch of the Loire Valley between Angers and Tours. Here lay not only Saumur and Chinon, the latter the great castle-treasury where John spent more time than any other single place in these years, but also the abbey of Fontevraud, newly established as the mausoleum of the Angevin dynasty. Here were buried John's father Henry, his brother Richard and his sister Joan: in 1204 John's mother Eleanor was also laid to rest here, followed later by his widow, Isabella of Angoulême, and his nephew, Raymond VII of Toulouse. When John lost Anjou and Normandy he lost not only two provinces, he lost also the two main nuclei of power and sentiment in the whole Angevin Empire.

## PROVINCIAL ADMINISTRATION

Since an itinerant king was normally absent from any given province, the work of organizing and directing local administration had to be undertaken by somebody else. The more regularly the accounts of *prévôts* and *baillis* were checked the better. Judicial affairs also needed regular attention. They could not efficiently be delayed until the ruler's next visit. The king-duke required the services of a permanent representative equipped with full powers to act on his master's behalf. Whenever possible, most rulers seem to have preferred to use members of their own family for these purposes.

Following in this tradition, Henry II used his wife (especially before 1160), his eldest son (from 1170 to 1172) and perhaps also his mother, the Empress Matilda, as regents of England during his own absences abroad in the years before the great revolt of 1173–74. In Aquitaine Eleanor's uncle Ralph de Faye was described as procurator in 1163, but here the obvious ruler was the queen-duchess herself. Frequently, however, such royal regents were heads of government in name only. Anything else indeed would almost certainly have worried a ruler determined, as Henry was, to keep the reins of power in his own hands. Thus in the fifty years between 1154 and 1204 there were probably only three or four periods when a member of the royal family was also an effective head of government: Geoffrey of Brittany from 1181 to his death in 1186; Richard in Aquitaine from 1175 to 1189; Eleanor in Aquitaine in 1199 and possibly also between 1168 and 1172. John never got a look in except in Ireland in 1185 (though he hoped to in 1191–92 while Richard was away on crusade). As for Henry II's eldest son, the Young King Henry, he was condemned to ineffectiveness partly in consequence of the defects of his own character and partly because he had the misfortune, as heir apparent to the patrimony, England, Normandy and Anjou, to live too much in his father's shadow.

As these details suggest, it is not the case that Henry used his family until it betrayed him in the great war of 1173–74 and that subsequently he turned to the administrators who had saved him in that crisis. There was no sudden reversal of policy. If anything, he used his family more after 1173–74 than he had before. Since his sons were growing older all the time this is, of course, hardly surprising, though perhaps not immediately apparent to the historian who concentrates on England alone. In this context the real change came when the deaths of the Young King (1183), Geoffrey (1186) and Henry II himself (1189) meant that the ruling dynasty was once more short of adult males. That Richard should choose to overlook John was only natural. John had been lord of Ireland since 1177 and his brief and inglorious performance there in 1185 was hardly designed to encourage Richard to give him wider responsibilities. In any event, as Henry II's behaviour indicates, kings tended to be kinder to their sons than to their younger brothers.

Given the continuous pressure of basic political and administrative problems and the only occasional availability of members of the royal family capable of coping with them, it was probably inevitable that strong centralized systems of government would develop in each of the provinces of the empire. We can best see the system working in England. Here the exchequer functioned as an authoritative and effective organ of government, not merely a financial department but an office of general administration. By the 1170s the exchequer staff had taken up permanent residence at Westminster. When the king was in the realm there were close links, indeed a marked degree of overlap, both in business and personnel, between exchequer and household. When the king was away, work went on very much as usual, most of it authorized by writs sealed with the justiciar's personal seal. Occasionally the king intervened, sending written instructions from overseas, *brevia de ultra mare,* but essentially the donkey-work of central supervision of law enforcement, dispute settlement, estate management, forest and castle maintenance went on regardless. It did so not only when the king was in France; it did so also while he was much further away still, on crusade in the Holy Land or in prison in Germany. Even the highly political business of patronage, man management, could be carried on by the justiciar, subject always, of course, to the possibility of overriding royal action.

Exchequers also existed in Normandy and (from 1200) in Ireland; in other provinces there is no evidence that they did. On the other hand, each seneschal clearly had his own household staff who were as capable of auditing accounts as they were of dealing with business, whether judicial, military or managerial. In 1204, when Philip Augustus set out the functions and perquisites of the seneschals of Poitou and Anjou in charters granting these offices to Aimeri of Thouars and William des Roches, he stipulated that whenever he levied a *demanda* or a *tallia* it would be up to the seneschal to collect it and to produce a proper written account. The justiciar/seneschal was appointed at the king's pleasure and could be removed from office, or transferred, whenever the ruler chose.

The career of Robert of Thornham is an instructive one. He accompanied Richard on crusade and was appointed co-governor of Cyprus. After the king's return Robert became seneschal of Anjou (1195–99) and was active in the affairs of Brittany. In 1201 John reappointed him seneschal, initially for the whole of Aquitaine (Poitou and Gascony), but then, though somewhat apologetically, cut his jurisdiction by appointing Martin Algais as seneschal of Gascony and Perigord. Since Robert of Thornham was an English layman, and indeed not of baronial rank, it is clear that his authority in Anjou and Aquitaine depended entirely on his position as an official at the head of a royal system of provincial government. Just how well the system could work was shown by its remarkably smooth functioning during Richard's absence on crusade (see above p. 43).

## PATRONAGE

Despite bureaucratic growth both at the centre and in the provinces, political stability still depended primarily on the ruler's ability to manage a small but immensely powerful aristocratic establishment. How was this to be done? The vital element here was the extent to which the ruler was able to exercise control over inheritances and marriages. In England and Normandy this was an area in which the Angevins inherited well-defined rights which their predecessors had long enjoyed. In other provinces the position was not so clear-cut. Understandably, wealthy families liked to arrange these matters for themselves, and claimed the right to do so, but increasingly they found they had to give way before a prince who, if necessary, could call upon the financial and military resources of his whole empire. This meant that the ruler's powers of patronage were immense. He not only had offices – both secular and ecclesiastical – at his disposal, he also had heirs, heiresses and widows. In 1156, for example, Henry took the young viscount of Limoges out of the custody of his uncle and arranged his marriage to Sarah, daughter of Earl Reginald of Cornwall. In 1177 Henry treated the richest heiress in Berry, Denise daughter of the lord of Châteauroux and Déols, in the same way, eventually giving her in marriage to an Anglo-Norman noble, Baldwin de Redvers. Then, after she was widowed, he offered to give her first to William Marshal and then to Baldwin of Béthune. However, as was his way, he kept them waiting, and when he died in July 1189 Denise was still in his custody.[7] Meanwhile Richard, in revolt against his father, had promised her to one of his own companions-in-arms, Andrew de Chauvigny and he had no sooner come to the throne than he fulfilled this promise; later, in 1195, he compensated Baldwin of Béthune with another rich widow, Hawisa countess of Aumale (northeast Normandy) and lady of Holderness (north-east England). Richard also provided for his illegitimate son Philip in the same way, giving him the heiress to the lordship of Cognac.

Patronage on this scale was extremely lucrative. Men offered money in order to obtain what the king had to offer: offices (from the chancellorship down), succession to estates, custody of land, wardship and marriage. All of these were to be had at a price and the

---

7　N. Vincent, 'William Marshal, King Henry II and the honour of Châteauroux', *Archives* 25 (2000), 1–14.

price was negotiable. John, for example, accepted 1,000 *livres poitevins* for custody of the heir to the lordship of Blanquefort (near Bordeaux). Here was an area in which a king could hope to raise more money by consistently driving harder bargains. Thus it was in the king's interest to compile records which told him just how rich his tenants were – for example, the 'Roll of ladies, boys and girls' produced by Henry II's administrators in England. It is clear that ambitious men frequently offered more than they could afford. The expectation was that, so long as they served the king loyally, they would not actually be required to pay more than a small proportion of their offer. This expectation had the effect of encouraging men to bid highly. But a man who fell out of favour would find that he had to pay up promptly – or get into even worse trouble. In John's reign this was the fate which befell William de Braose and his family. In other words by offering these people what they wanted – though at a price – and by fining them heavily when they were in political difficulties, the king had found a practical method of soaking the rich. Yet clearly this was not just a way of making money; it was also a system of political control. It is not surprising that the king's court was the focal point of the whole political system; a turbulent, lively, tense, factious place in which men – and a few women – pushed and jostled each other in desperate attempts to catch the ruler's eye. This is the context in which we should understand the advice on government which, according to Walter Map, Henry II received from his mother:

> He should spin out all the affairs of everyone, keep in his own hand all posts for as long as possible – collecting their revenues the while, and make the aspirants to them hang on in hope. She supported this advice with an unkind parable: an unruly hawk, if meat is often offered to it, then snatched away or hid becomes keener and more inclined towards attentiveness and obedience'.[8]

In these circumstances patronage was one of the strongest cards in the king's hand. It mattered how he played it, and a king who played it badly would soon find himself in trouble.

## ROYAL AND PROVINCIAL CUSTOM

The Angevin Empire was to prove much more ephemeral than the individual provinces of which it was comprised. For this reason

8 Walter Map *Courtiers' Trifles*, p. 479.

historians are very conscious of the strength of provincial custom. Not surprisingly this means that legal historians incline to the view that England was ruled by English custom, Normandy by Norman custom, Anjou by Angevin custom, Poitou by Poitevin custom, and so on. It is said indeed that not only was this done but also that it was done deliberately. On his deathbed Henry II's father is supposed to have forbidden his son to introduce Norman or English customs into Anjou or vice versa. This is regarded as 'a fundamental principle of the Angevin empire'[9] and one that became steadily harder to tamper with as twelfth- and thirteenth-century legal developments meant that regional custom came to be more precisely defined, more often written down and in this way stabilized, 'crystallized'.

Did this 'fundamental principle' ever really exist? All that we can safely infer from Geoffrey Plantagenet's famous last words is that our informant, John of Marmoutier, writing *c*.1170, believed either that such introductions had already occurred or that they were likely to occur. And perhaps the monk of Marmoutier (Tours) was right to be concerned. Boussard's study of the office of seneschal in Anjou led him to the conclusion that the county was losing its individuality and being merged into the ensemble of Angevin territories,[10] a development highlighted by the appointment of the Englishman Robert of Thornham as seneschal of Anjou in 1195. Ralph of Diceto's account of how the young Philip Augustus was advised to copy the methods which Henry used to govern England strongly suggests that in English court circles English methods of government were thought good enough to introduce anywhere. It can come as no surprise, first of all, that in 1210 John enunciated the principle that English laws and customs should be observed in his lordship of Ireland, and second, that other evidence shows that many English procedures were already in operation in Ireland prior to 1210.

Perhaps Ireland was a special case. On the other hand, French legal historians believe that medieval Norman law possessed a special quality deriving from its long association with England. Perhaps, then, we have two special cases. But just how 'special' was Norman law? To Jean Yver, taking a broad view, it seemed that Norman custom belonged within a Western – or Plantagenet – group which included the customs of Brittany, Maine, Anjou, Touraine and

---

9 J. Le Patourel, *The Norman Empire* (Oxford, 1976), p. 276.
10 J. Boussard, *Le comté d'Anjou sous Henri Plantegenêt et ses fils, 1151–1204* (Paris, 1938).

Poitou;[11] a group which was clearly different from the customs of eastern – or Capetian – France. Taking a broader view still, Paul Hyams has argued that even the common law of England, English as roast beef though it may be, should none the less be placed firmly in Yver's 'group of customs of the West'.[12] Even if the king merely wished to ensure that lords enforced their own local custom 'properly', the likelihood is that if the king had power enough then his definition of what was 'proper' would be the one which carried weight. In that case, royal jurisdiction would tend to result in similar procedures and similar devices being adopted in the different provinces. Against this it has to be said that only two clearcut cases of what has been called 'imperial legislation'[13] – edicts intended to apply to the whole empire – have been found: the edict of Verneuil of 1177 and the Assize of Arms of 1181. Moreover most historians would still argue that Anglo-Norman custom was significantly different from the rest of the western group. But this conclusion is very largely based on a study of western custumals which date from the second half of the thirteenth century or later and which are not necessarily the safest guides to practice 50 years or more earlier. There is indeed clear charter and chronicle evidence that the custom which legal historians regard as being Anglo-Norman *par excellence*, i.e. the custom of seigneurial wardship, was applied throughout their dominions by all three Angevin kings (see pp. 78–9) – despite the fact that there is no surviving evidence of any legislation requiring this. (In the absence of contemporary legal literature from the lands south of Normandy one would not really expect to find any.) In 1185 Duke Geoffrey issued an assize regulating succession to baronies and knight's fees in Brittany, regulating wardship and relief, establishing primogeniture, and opening a loophole for the application of seigneurial wardship in those cases where the deceased left no living brothers. It begins to look, in other words, as though we are faced not with a number of special cases but with a body of custom which is tending towards an approximate uniformity throughout the whole of the Angevin Empire. In the case of seigneurial wardship it is crystal clear that this was largely the result of determined government

11 J. Yver, 'Les caractères originaux de coutumes de l'ouest de la France', *Revue d'histoire de droit français et étranger*, 4th series, 30 (1952).
12 P. Hyams, 'The common law and the French connection', in R. A. Brown (ed.), *Proceedings of the Battle Conference on Anglo-Norman Studies*, 4, 1981 (Woodbridge, 1982).
13 J. C. Holt, 'The end of the Anglo-Norman realm', *Proceedings of the British Academy*, 61 (1975), reprinted in *Magna Carta and Medieval Government* (London, 1985).

action, the power of the ruler to overcome opposition and push regional variants in the direction of legal uniformity. Moreover, administrative responses to new challenges such as the need to raise money on a new scale in the hope of recovering Jerusalem after its capture by Saladin (1187) also tended in the direction of uniformity; the same measures were adopted everywhere for the collection of the Saladin Tithe.[14]

## COHESION?

The development of centralized systems of provincial government did not mean that each province was treated as an autonomous unit which went its own way, regardless of the others. On the contrary, the chancery rolls of the early years of John's reign testify to a complex system of inter-provincial administrative links. Even the two most highly developed of the provincial bureaucracies, the exchequers of England and Normandy, maintained a close working relationship. And above it all went the king itinerating ceaselessly over the length and breadth of his dominions. When the king was in the country household government reinforced provincial government and made it more burdensome. (The government of England became particularly oppressive after 1203 when John was very largely confined to one province.) But even after the king had moved on there were several ways in which his impact could still be felt.

In the first place it often happened that a member of the king's household stayed behind in order to take over provincial or local office. In some cases this meant that a courtier had come home, but in others it meant the appointment of an outsider. William Longchamp, for example, a Norman by birth, who became Richard's chancellor while he was duke of Aquitaine, retained that office after 1189 and then acted as justiciar in England in 1190–91. In 1176 an Englishman, Richard of Ilchester, was made seneschal of Normandy, and in the 1180s other 'outsiders' can be found acting at lower levels of Norman administration: Richard of Cardiff and Geoffrey of Ripon as *baillis*, while Robert 'the Angevin' – presumably a man from Anjou – held both the *vicomté* of the Cotentin and the *prévoté* of Barfleur – a vital cross-Channel port. Given the strength of ties of kinship and neighbourhood, given too the well-articulated sentiment

14 J. Dunbabin, *France in the Making 843–1180* (Oxford, 1985), p. 348.

in favour of local men being appointed to local office, it was only to be expected that an outsider would have his problems. In 1191 these problems contributed to Longchamp's downfall but circumstances then were peculiar (John plotting while Richard was away on crusade). Other men's careers show that such problems could be overcome: the career of Robert of Thornham, for example (see p. 77). When Richard I died, it was Robert of Thornham, as seneschal of Anjou, who opened the gates of Chinon to admit John. In 1204–5, as seneschal of Poitou, his hard-fought defence of the province won the unstinting praise of Ralph of Coggeshall. Later in John's reign two more Englishmen were appointed seneschal of Poitou: Hubert de Burgh (who had won fame as the defender of Chinon in 1205) and Geoffrey de Neville. Indeed, by 1220 the mayor and commune of Niort were insistent that they wanted an Englishman as seneschal – in preference to a member of the local aristocracy whom they perceived as a threat to their interests (see pp. 64, 110).

This, of course, is the context in which we must set John's notorious employment of 'foreigners' in England. Some of them – the kindred of Gerard d'Athée (from the Touraine) who earned a dubious immortality in clause 50 of Magna Carta, for example – were chiefly employed in John's corps of strong-arm agents. Yet not all of those who flocked to England after John lost the continental territories in which they had previously made their careers can be pigeon-holed as 'mercenary captains' whose birth made them the target of aristocratic sneers. Peter des Roches, for example, was both a financial expert and of aristocratic birth, a relative of William des Roches, the seneschal of Anjou who played such a crucial role in 1199–1203. Peter began his career in Richard's household. Under John he was attached to the chamber staff, and became one of the very few men whom that king really trusted. In 1205 he was rewarded with the rich see of Winchester. He held the office of justiciar in 1213–14, enjoyed immense power in the early years of Henry III's reign and ended his life as a man of European reputation (with the Emperor Frederick he rode into Jerusalem in 1229).

The careers of Longchamp (bishop of Ely 1189–97) and des Roches (bishop of Winchester 1205–38) serve to remind us that the king's ecclesiastical patronage also enabled him to move men from province to province. In this field of action canon law could occasionally be a stumbling block. In 1158, for example, the canons of Bordeaux found they could not agree on a new archbishop and so the suffragan bishops were invited to make the choice. Henry II had a candidate of his own to promote and he joined their deliberations. Bishop Hugh of Angoulême, however, refused to proceed with the election while the king was present. Henry, outfaced, had to withdraw and someone else was elected. But the whole point of the story, told by a clerk of the church of Angoulême, was to celebrate one man's remarkable courage. As a rule electors were pliable. Even in this case we find that Henry's defeated candidate was immediately consoled with another bishopric (Perigueux). Indeed, the next two archbishops of Bordeaux, Hardouin, formerly dean of Le Mans (elected in 1160), and William, formerly abbot of Reading (elected in 1173), were both 'outsiders' who clearly owed their advancement to royal favour.

These examples – which could easily be multiplied – suggest that the coherence of the Angevin Empire was a question of people as well as a question of formal administrative structures. A similar effect was achieved when the custody of a minor or the hand of an heiress, two of local society's most precious assets, were given to men from outside the province. In 1156, for example, custody of the viscount of Limoges (see p. 78) was granted jointly to William Pandolf, an Anglo-Norman, and Geoffrey de Neufbourg, brother of the count of Perche. In 1190 Richard gave Hawisa countess of Aumale in marriage to William de Fors, a Poitevin who was one of the commanders of his crusading fleet (see p. 78 for her next marriage). Just as office-holders, both clerks and laymen, could be transferred from one province to another, so also men with influence at court – *familiares* – were likely to find themselves holding estates in several different provinces at once. In these ways the incessant movement of the itinerant court posed a constant threat to long-cherished provincial autonomy. Naturally this was a process which caused friction; disappointed men could appeal to local sentiment and be sure of a sympathetic hearing. A Poitevin aristocrat, Hugh of Chauvigny, is reported to have hated all Englishmen and there is plenty of evidence to show that the feeling was mutual. None the less, there are two points worth making. First, in the history of the Angevin Empire there was never a period when it was obvious that the whole empire was being run in the interests of just one regional group – as was the case with the Norman Empire in the generation after 1066. Second, there is no reason to think that either provincial solidarity or provincial resentment of outsiders played a significant role in the collapse of 1203–4. By this date the process which might have resulted in the creation of a single supra-provincial aristocracy for the empire as a whole, the kind of elite which a historian of Carolingian Europe might call a *Reichsadel,* was still in its early stages. Only in one sector of the empire did such an elite exist: in the old Anglo-Norman realm. In 1204 there were still more than a hundred Norman tenants-in-chief who also held land in England. A man like Walter of Coutances, simultaneously archdeacon of Oxford and treasurer of Rouen, then bishop of Lincoln (1183–84), and finally archbishop of Rouen (1185–1207), seems to have moved effortlessly between the two churches. In 1204 at the highest social level there were still many like Walter, or like William Marshal, who were Anglo-Norman rather than either English or Norman. Yet the two most closely linked provinces were split apart in the débâcle of 1203–4, while the two provinces with the weakest family, tenurial and administrative ties, England and Gascony, were the ones which stayed together much the longest.

The contrast is, of course, one which is easily explained. Normandy was lost in 1203–4, as was Anjou, because it was here – and not against Poitou or Gascony – that Philip concentrated his attack. But an explanation couched in these terms implies that structural factors – problems of social, administrative or even mental cohesiveness – counted for less than the contingencies of war and politics. The most important component of Angevin government was the king himself. And John was, as Sellar and Yeatman put it, 'an awful king'.[15]

---

15  W. C. Sellar and R. J. Yeatman, *1066 and All That* (London, 1930), p. 24.

# 7 The crisis of the Angevin Empire, 1199–1206

The Christmas of 1204 must have been a cheerless feast for King John. For him the history of the last two years had been one long catalogue of disaster, far worse than is implied by the words 'the loss of Normandy' – the label which is conventionally attached to these events. Of the vast Plantagenet territories on the Continent only a pitiful remnant was still in his hands. In Normandy nothing; in Anjou, Maine and Touraine only two isolated fortresses, Chinon and Loches, still held out; in Poitou, apart from his wife's county of Angoulême, only La Rochelle and Oléron; in Gascony only a handful of towns, Bordeaux, Bayonne, Bazas, St-Émilion and La Réole. In Normandy, Anjou, Maine, Touraine and Poitou most men recognized Philip Augustus as their new lord; in Gascony they acknowledged Alfonso VIII of Castile. Given the tide of events in 1203 and 1204 it seemed to be just a matter of time before the last outposts fell, leaving John with nothing but his island kingdom and his lordship over Ireland. Indeed, even England seemed to be in jeopardy. There was, John feared, a rebellious confederation between Ranulf, earl of Chester, and Gwenwynwyn, prince of Powys. Still more alarming was the prospect of the invasion of England which Philip of France was known to be planning. The entire Angevin Empire seemed to be tumbling like a house of cards. Why was this happening? Was John faced by insuperable problems – or was the collapse simply the result of his own inadequacies? In trying to answer this question it is helpful to begin with a survey of events.

## THE WAR OF ANGEVIN SUCCESSION

In the history of the Angevin Empire the death of Richard I, on 6 April, was the first of two critical events that occurred in 1199. At the court of King Philip of France it was regarded as providential – and with good reason. Politically and militarily Philip had been no match for his Plantagenet rival. Ever since 1194 Richard had steadily pushed forward, forcing Philip to hand back the lands and castles he had seized during Richard's captivity. But at the siege of Chalus-Chabrol a moment's carelessness cost Richard his life. His unexpected death changed everything.

To begin with, it precipitated simultaneously both a Capetian invasion of Normandy and a succession dispute. Immediately upon hearing the news of Richard's fatal injury, Philip invaded and seized Evreux. John's first move was to take control of the treasury and castle of Chinon; but the barons of Anjou, Maine and Touraine led by William des Roches, Juhel de Mayenne and Robert de Vitré decided that, in accordance with Angevin custom, they preferred the son of an elder brother (i.e. Arthur, son of Geoffrey) to a younger brother (John). In return for sweeping concessions from Arthur and his mother Constance they declared in favour of the 12-year-old boy and, naturally, found willing support from Philip. Driven out of Anjou and with the additional threat of a Scottish invasion of England to contend with, John acted swiftly to get his authority recognized in Normandy and England. On 25 April he was invested as duke at Rouen. Thanks to the measures taken by his envoys to England, Hubert Walter and William Marshal, he faced no further opposition and was crowned king at Westminster on 27 May.

In the crisis of April 1199 John relied on his mother, whose right to Aquitaine not even Philip could dispute, to ensure the loyalty of the lords of Poitou. She granted the lordship of Ste-Sévère to Andrew of Chauvigny and the ducal castles of Talmont and Benon to Ralph of Mauléon. In the struggle for Anjou John owed much to the political and military pressure which the Poitevins then exercised on his behalf. Foremost among them were the families of Lusignan and Thouars. It was Aimeri viscount of Thouars and the three senior Lusignans (Hugh of Lusignan, his brother Ralph of Exoudun count of Eu and their uncle Geoffrey) who, late in May 1199, attacked Tours in an attempt to capture Arthur. Aimeri of Thouars, described by a Tours chronicler as 'an eloquent and famous man, the outstanding representative of his house', was John's choice as seneschal of Anjou in opposition to Arthur's and Philip's nominee, William des Roches.

In June John returned to Normandy and made a truce with Philip. He used the truce to confirm the alliances he had inherited from

Richard, notably with the counts of Flanders and Boulogne, and with Otto IV. In all no fewer than 15 French counts swore to help John, if necessary against the king of France. In September he advanced into Maine in force, driving Philip before him. His position was now so strong that William des Roches decided to switch sides. He met John at Le Mans and swore an oath of allegiance to him. Better than that, he brought Constance and Arthur with him. The successsion dispute, it seemed, had been settled, and entirely in John's favour. This was a very great triumph, and the price that William presumably demanded, the dismissal of Aimeri de Thouars from authority in Anjou, a small one in the circumstances.

But during the following night Arthur, Constance and Aimeri fled, first to Angers and then to Philip's court. Within the space of a few hours the triumph had crumbled. What had happened to precipitate so sudden a lurch of fortune's wheel? According to Roger of Howden, someone had told Arthur that John intended to put him in prison. In 1202 Arthur was indeed imprisoned by John, and – it was generally thought, almost certainly correctly – was then murdered on his orders. But since Howden died in 1201, his account of 1199 cannot possibly have been influenced by this notorious scandal. Presumably John's record of treachery – to his father in 1189, to his brother in 1193–94, to King Philip in 1194 – was already such that Arthur and his advisers felt that the warning they received at Le Mans in September 1199 was one they had to take seriously. Over the next few months John's position deteriorated further. A number of the great nobles of northern France decided that the time had come to go on crusade, among them the counts of Flanders and Perche. As Philip's court historian, William the Breton, remembered it, the counts of Flanders, Blois and Perche and other princes who had deserted Philip, took the cross when they realized that Richard's death had deprived them of aid and counsel. In fact, as we have seen, as late as the summer of 1199 they had been prepared to remain true to the Angevin alliance which Richard had established in 1197–98. They began to take the cross not immediately after his death in April but in November. It is hard to account for the timing of this change of mind on the part of 'those princes who had deserted Philip' except in terms of their understanding of the political implications of the sudden volte-face by Arthur and the viscount of Thouars. Their dramatic night departure from John's court was thus the second decisive moment of 1199.

Soon after Christmas 1199 John met Philip Augustus and

conceded the terms which were then finalized in the treaty of Le Goulet (May 1200). By this John agreed that Philip was entitled to retain the territory – the Evrécin – he had conquered in Normandy; he made concessions to Philip in Auvergne and Berry, not only Issoudun and Graçay but also Déols and Châteauroux, the fiefs of Andrew de Chauvigny – a concession which suggests that Andrew too had abandoned John late in 1199. In return Philip recognized John as Richard's lawful heir, in Anjou as well as in the other Angevin dominions in France. For this John agreed to pay Philip a relief of 20,000 marks. It was the first time that a relief was paid, that an Angevin ruler had acknowledged the formal right of his over-lord the king of France in this concrete and expensive fashion. But at least the succession dispute of 1199 had been settled in John's favour and he may well have felt that all this, plus the hostility of Thouars, was a small price to pay for the support of William des Roches and the acquisition of Anjou. Philip stood aside as John occupied Angers in June 1200, taking 150 hostages from the city as a pledge of its doubtful loyalty. He then visited Aquitaine in force, and no one stood against him. Apart from the concessions made at Le Goulet, he had now, in the words of the annalist of St Aubin at Angers, 'obtained the whole realm that had belonged to his father as far as the Cross of Charlemagne'. And no doubt the hard-pressed tax-payers in both Angevin and Capetian dominions welcomed the peace between their kings.

John, however, was now diplomatically isolated. In the treaty of Le Goulet he had promised to give no support of any kind to Otto, nor aid to the count of Flanders or to any of king of France's subjects in any action they undertook against Philip.

## THE REVOLT OF THE LUSIGNANS, 1201–2

On 24 August 1200 John married Isabella, the daughter and heiress of Count Audemar of Angoulême. In the opinion of most contemporary chroniclers this was the decisive mistake. Yet in view of Angoulême's wealth and strategic importance – astride the vital lines of communication between Poitiers and Bordeaux – there was much to be said in favour of this marriage. The problem was that Isabella was already promised to someone else: to Hugh of Lusignan. According to Roger of Howden, this had been a betrothal arranged by King Richard. Since the houses of Angoulême and Lusignan had both laid claim to La Marche since 1177, it could be that Richard had seen this betrothal as a means of reconciling the two of them to the fact of his continuing retention of La Marche. But if this is so, it had failed to prevent Audemar from joining the rebellion of Aimar of Limoges and seeking King Philip's support for his claim. Then, as late in 1199 John's former allies abandoned him, Hugh of Lusignan saw an opportunity. According to Bernard Itier, a well-informed Limousin contemporary, he seized the disputed county – indeed, according to a later chronicler, he even kidnapped Eleanor of Aquitaine – and John evidently felt that at this juncture he had little choice but to accept a *fait accompli*. By January 1200 he had recognized Hugh as Count of La Marche. If John faced no opposition in Aquitaine in the summer of 1200 it was probably because he had both acquiesced in this extension of Lusignan power and had made Audemar of Angoulême an offer he could hardly resist.

Undoubtedly Hugh's acquisition of La Marche meant that John could not afford to let Hugh and Isabella marry. So massive a power bloc as the union of Lusignan, La Marche and Angoulême threatened to be disastrous for ducal authority in Poitou. In these circumstances it made good political sense for John, who had already had his first marriage annulled, to marry Isabella himself. Hugh was understandably irritated at being deprived of the prospect of succeeding to Angoulême. Perhaps, suitably compensated, he might have become reconciled to the loss, but it may be that John was still smarting over the way in which Hugh had got his hands on La Marche. At any rate the king clearly had not the slightest intention of placating Hugh and his kindred now. On the contrary, his promise to include the vitally important strongholds of Niort and Saintes in his new wife's dower can only have served to further exasperate Hugh. In the spring of 1201 John ordered the confiscation of La Marche (which he then granted to his new father-in-law Count Audemar) and of the lands which Ralph of Exoudun held in Normandy. His subsequent treatment of the Lusignans' pleas for justice led to them appealing to the king of France (autumn 1201). Philip then summoned John before his court. John's refusal to attend resulted in the king of France pronouncing the confiscation of all John's fiefs (April 1202). Philip accepted Arthur's homage for Poitou, Anjou, Maine and Touraine and arranged for Arthur to marry his daughter Mary. Thus the Lusignan revolt led directly to the reopening of the war of Angevin succession.

As early as the spring of 1201 Eleanor of Aquitaine had seen which way the wind was blowing and, though she was then 80 years of age and in retreat at Fontevraud, she took steps to counterbalance the loss of Lusignan support. Summoning Aimeri of Thouars to her side she persuaded him to forget his grudge against John. Finally a form of reconciliation between king and viscount was worked out. But John was, as always, suspicious. He demanded guarantees, including the handing over of Aimeri's son Geoffrey as a hostage. Similarly in October 1201 John made terms with Juhel of Mayenne, giving him the castles he claimed (confirming the grants that Arthur had made in 1199) and again exacting hostages. Whatever the value of these precarious friendships may have been, they failed to prevent Arthur and the Lusignans from launching a determined attack on John's position in Poitou in 1202. Although John acquired the lands of Audemar of Angoulême when the count died on 16 June 1202, in other respects his position remained weak. He still lacked allies. The counts of Flanders, Blois and Perche had now left for the East (the Fourth Crusade), while the counts of Toulouse and Boulogne had either already gone over to Philip or were on the point of doing so. The only prince to be interested in friendship with John at this time was Sancho of Navarre: but in February 1202, when their alliance was sealed, Sancho was more in need of assistance than able to provide it.

In May Philip invaded Normandy and, unimpeded by John, captured a number of castles on Normandy's eastern frontier: Boutavant, Eu, Aumale, Drincourt, Mortemer, Lions-la-Forêt and Gournay. Arthur met the Lusignans and their friends at a rendezvous at Tours. John moved south to meet this threat and was at Le Mans on 30 July 1202 when he heard that Arthur had managed to trap his mother in the castle of Mirebeau, nearly 100 miles to the south. For once in his life John moved with such decisive speed that he was able to turn the tables. At dawn on 1 August his troops led by William des Roches and Aimeri of Thouars took his enemies by surprise. Not a single rebel escaped. 'God be praised for our happy success', wrote John in the report of his victory which he sent to England. More than 200 knights were captured, at their head Arthur, Hugh and Geoffrey of Lusignan, Andrew de Chauvigny, the viscount of Châtellerault and some members of other Poitevin baronial houses, notably Thouars and Mauléon. It was undoubtedly a resounding triumph. Richard had boasted extravagantly when he captured less than 100 French knights at Gisors in 1198. Soon afterwards John's position was further strengthened when the viscount of Limoges was taken prisoner and sent to Chinon. In the summer of 1202 it looked at though John had defeated his enemies more decisively than ever his father or brother had been able to do. Yet within two years he had contrived to lose both Anjou and Normandy.

## DEFEAT ON ALL FRONTS, 1202–4

Part of the problem was that John 'could not resist the temptation to kick a man when he was down'.[1] A victory like that at Mirebeau brought massive temptations in its wake and John succumbed massively. His most serious offence was his responsibility for Arthur's murder, but his treatment of all the prisoners was widely regarded as being intolerably harsh. Since there was hardly a noble in Poitou who did not have a kinsman or a friend among the knights taken at Mirebeau this meant that John managed to offend almost the entire aristocracy, including some powerful barons, like William of Mauléon, not hitherto involved in the revolt of the Lusignans. Moreover, those who felt they had contributed most to John's victory, William des Roches and Aimeri of Thouars, were particularly angry when John denied them any say in deciding the prisoners' fate. In September 1202, only a few weeks after they had fought at John's side at Mirebeau, they rebelled against him – by now Aimeri's hostage son had been released – and in October they captured Angers. Soon they were joined by those lords with Breton connections who were made uneasy by the rumours of Arthur's fate: the lords of Mayenne, Craon, and Fougères. In November 1202 John begged the viscount of Beaumont not to believe those who said he had been speaking ill of him. But in January 1203 when Robert, count of Sées, on whose loyalty John had counted, handed Alençon over to Philip, the viscount followed him into revolt. The manner in which John had exploited his victory at Mirebeau meant that six months later he had virtually no friends anywhere in Poitou, Anjou, Maine and Touraine. With the defection of Robert of Sées, rebellion spread into southern Normandy. Garrisons held out in the citadel at Tours (until 1204) and in the great strongholds of Chinon and Loches (until 1205). John himself spent a few days in Le Mans in January 1203. Thereafter he stayed in Normandy and watched from afar while the central lands of the Angevin Empire were torn from

---

1  W. L. Warren, *King John* (London, 1961), p. 87.

his grasp. The last reference to an Angevin seneschal of Anjou is dated 16 April 1203; in this month it was Philip Augustus, not John, who cruised down the Loire and took possession of Saumur.

Then it was Normandy's turn. In the early summer of 1203 Philip resumed his attack. Great barrel loads of English money continued to be sent across the Channel – at least £30,000 between the autumn of 1201 and the end of 1203 – and John himself stayed in Normandy for almost the whole of 1203. Unfortunately he was hardly the most inspiring of leaders. In June the great fortress of Vaudreuil, guarding the approaches to Rouen on the left bank of the Seine, surrendered without a fight; John, though he was nearby, made no effort to relieve it. Indeed, he announced that this had been done on his orders. In August he laid siege to Alençon, where he hoped to capture both Robert of Sées and Juhel de Mayenne, but he retreated when Philip arrived unexpectedly with a hastily mustered force. Philip then turned against the strategically crucial military complex of Les Andelys. In late August John tried to dislodge the Capetian forces, but the attempt ended in utter confusion, and in that confusion his troops – he was not there himself – lost control of both Petit-Andeli and the Isle of Andeli. After that débâcle he left the fortress of Château-Gaillard to its own devices, making no further effort either to relieve the castle or harass the blockading French troops. For over five months the great castle on the rock held firm against a combination of attrition and fierce assault while John stayed almost entirely in the west of Normandy before finally leaving for England on 5 December 1203. In the next few months he talked about returning to Normandy and made a few gestures, but he sent little or no money there and did nothing effective.

On 6 March 1204 the courageous and exhausted garrison of Château-Gaillard surrendered. William the Breton, an eyewitness of the siege, identified as the fatal flaw in the castle's design a chapel which John had added and which allowed the French to force their way into the second ward. After that only Rouen and Arques were prepared to resist; everywhere else surrendered quickly. In May Philip swept through central Normandy, taking Argentan, Falaise, Caen, Bayeux and Lisieux in just three weeks. At the same time a force of Bretons captured Mont-St-Michel and Avranches. In Normandy, as in Anjou, there was hardly anyone who would fight for John. On 24 June 1204 the city of Rouen opened its gates to receive its new lord. Philip destroyed the former ducal castle within the town and built a large new one on a site which dominated the old city.

In the southwest the death of Eleanor of Aquitaine, on 31 March 1204, was the sign for a great rush to the Capetian court as the lords, prelates and towns of most of Poitou, including Saintonge and Perigord, hurried to do homage to the king of France. While Eleanor had lived men might reject John but hope to remain loyal to her. When she died, the flood gates were opened. In August 1204, fresh from his triumphs in Normandy, Philip visited Poitiers. In the words of Alfred Richard, 'le pays s'est donné, il n'a pas été conquis'.[2] In Gascony too the death of the old duchess was to have momentous consequences (see p. 30). More than thirty years earlier, in 1170, Henry II had given Gascony as a dowry to his daughter Eleanor on the occasion of her marriage to Alfonso VIII of Castile. It had been agreed, however, that the gift was not to take effect until after the death of Eleanor's mother, Eleanor of Aquitaine. In 1204, to add to John's troubles, Alfonso moved in to take possession of his wife's inheritance. He secured the support of some of the most powerful Gascon lords: the count of Armagnac, the viscounts of Béarn, Tartas, Orthez and the bishops of Bayonne, Dax and Bazas. His troops overran the province and Castilian garrisons were even established on the north bank of the Gironde, at Blaye and Bourg. By Christmas 1204 from the Pyrenees to the Channel coast the Angevin Empire was in ruins.

## HOLDING THE LINE, 1205–6

In 1205 John suffered some further setbacks. After making massive preparation for an expedition to the Continent he was forced to cancel it in humiliating circumstances. The stubborn commanders of Chinon and Loches finally gave up the hopeless struggle. None the less, for the first time there were signs that the apparently relentless advance of his enemies might be halted. The threatened French invasion of England failed to materialize. The Channel Islands were recaptured. The Gascon towns, their resistance organized by a militant archbishop of Bordeaux, held out against Alfonso of Castile. On 29 April 1205 John wrote to thank them for their good service. By the end of the year the town of Niort in Poitou had returned to his allegiance. In the summer of 1206 John returned to the continent. He recovered the Saintonge, consolidated his hold on Isabella's county

2  A. Richard, *Histoire des comtes de Poitou, 778–1204* (Paris, 1903), ii, p. 449.

of Angoulême and, after a fortnight's siege of Bourg, drove the last Castilian garrison out of Gascony. In September he marched north, forded the Loire and set his army to ravage Anjou. Perhaps this was intended as the first stage in a campaign of reconquest, but when the news came that Philip Augustus was approaching with an army, John beat a hasty retreat. In October the two kings agreed to a two-year truce based on the status quo. For the moment the crisis was over. Normandy and the Loire Valley had been lost but Gascony and the south west of Poitou (Angoulême, Aunis and Saintonge) were saved. At least something had been salvaged from the wreckage.

## THE CAUSES OF DEFEAT

How are we to explain what had happened, first the collapse and then the partial recovery? What no one would deny is that John's own record in these years was a bad one. He was rarely to be found where he was most needed. Even the turning of the tide in Poitou and Gascony in 1205–6 was due much more to the efforts and the energy of Savari de Mauléon (as seneschal of Poitou) and Elie de Malmort (as archbishop of Bordeaux) than to the initiative of the king himself. What can be debated – and has been – is whether or not John was facing enormous odds. Was the Angevin Empire in poor shape even before he succeeded to the throne? Was John quite simply outgunned by a richer and more powerful opponent? A glance at the map would seem to suggest, on the face of it, that the Angevins were far richer than the Capetians. Yet this apparently obvious conclusion has been denied by some modern scholars. It has indeed been argued that one of the reasons for the Plantagenet failure was that their resources were inadequate. So it is with the question of the relative wealth of John and Philip Augustus that we must begin.

Unfortunately the fragmentary state of the records means that it is not possible to calculate precisely the financial resources of either of them: that is why it is a debatable question. On the Capetian side historians rely on the account for the financial year 1202–3 (approximately June 1202 to June 1203) – the earliest set of royal accounts to survive and for this reason commonly, if misleadingly, known as 'the first budget of the French monarchy'. So far as territories go, this seems to be fairly complete; it records revenues from every part of the royal domain from Arras in the north to Bourges in the south.

On the other hand, the account of 1202–3 was not designed to record every item of royal income and expenditure but merely to check the revenues collected and payment made by local officials (chiefly *prévôts* and *baillis*). This means that sums paid directly into the king's chamber were likely to slip through the net. So far as the Angevins are concerned, the position is even more awkward. In territorial terms the records are hopelessly incomplete. The evidence permits us to make more or less reasonable estimates of John's English, Irish and Norman revenues, but for Aquitaine and Anjou there are no extant accounts of any sort whatever. In these circumstances to calculate *recorded* revenue is an essential first step – but only a first step. John (certainly) and Philip Augustus (possibly) actually received much more than this. By 'recorded revenue' I mean the combined total of that year's treasury receipts and authorized expenditure. (Throughout I shall use approximations because to give the exact figures derived from the accounts would give a misleading impression of precision to what is essentially a very rough and ready exercise.)

The 1202–3 Capetian accounts record transactions to the value of aproximately 197,000 *livres parisis*. But this includes a sum of 59,375 *l.p.* transferred from the treasury in the Temple, which could well have been drawn from a reserve built up by Philip, but which at any rate should not be counted as part of that year's revenue. Deducting this leaves a net revenue for the year of 137,000 *l.p.*, equivalent to 198,500 *livres angevins*. This, it should be remembered, was a year when Philip's stock was high and when he was able to impose a war tax, the *prisée des sergeants* which brought in 27,000 *l.p.* By contrast, 1202–3 was a disastrous year for John. He had lost Anjou, Maine and Touraine and was fast losing territory in Normandy. The fragmentary Norman roll for 1202–3 tells its own story of collapse. According to recent estimates Norman revenues in 1202–3 were down to between 38 per cent and 45 per cent of 1198 levels.[3] A comparison of Philip's revenues in 1202–3 with John's revenues in that same year will not tell us anything about their relative wealth on the eve of war. A surviving tiny fragment of the Norman exchequer record for 1200–1 suggests that then John was still able to operate his brother's fiscal system which he was clearly in no position to do in 1202–3. Clearly, comparing Angevin and

---

3  V. Moss, 'The Norman Exchequer Rolls of King John', in S. Church (ed.), *King John: New Interpretations* (Woodbridge, 1999).

Capetian financial resources in 1202–3 is vital if we are trying to explain what happened during the course of that particular year. If, on the other hand, we are attempting a related but different exercise, trying to assess the underlying level of resources available to both Angevins and Capetians *c*.1200, then it would be more appropriate to compare like with like, i.e a good Capetian year with a good Angevin year: Philip's 1202–3 with Richard's 1197–98. In this case it would mean that against Philip's 198,500 *l. a.*, we should set a net English revenue (including a carucage) of about £26,500 (106,000 *l.a.*) plus a net Norman revenue of 98,000 *l.a.* (this is the 1198 total less the revenue from Evreux, ceded to Philip by 1200). The combined total of 204,000 *l.a.* indicates that from England and Normandy alone the Angevins disposed of greater resources the Capetians – that is without counting Ireland, Anjou and Aquitaine.

What the 'ordinary' revenue of Ireland might have been *c*. 1200 is hard to say; the only Irish pipe roll of John's reign (for 1212) post-dates a period of drastic political change. But since from October 1203 to October 1204 John received at least £1,700 from, Ireland, a conservative estimate might be £1,500 (6,000 *l.a.*). What about the revenues from Anjou and Aquitaine? I have already pointed out (pp. 60–61) that revenues were there for the collecting and that they were collected. Against this it has been correctly noted that the earliest statements of royal revenue from Anjou and Poitou show that the income derived from these provinces was pitifully low. The earliest record for Anjou and Touraine is contained in the Capetian account for 1221 and it suggests that the king's annual income from here may have been only about £1,500; the equivalent for Poitou, the account for 1238, gives a figure of less than £1,500. But it would be rash to conclude that the Angevins received only some £3,000 from the whole of Anjou and Aquitaine. In the first place the revenues of Gascony should not be forgotten – even though, in all probability, these were fairly low in the days before the take-off of the Bordeaux wine trade. In the second place the earliest accounts for Anjou and Poitou both date from a period when the political structure of the two provinces was very different from what it had been in 1200. In August 1204 Philip made William des Roches hereditary seneschal of Anjou and then, in a further series of grants made in 1204 and 1206, he, in effect, handed Anjou over to him. In Maine the Angevins had held little except Le Mans itself and this Philip granted in 1204 to Richard's widow Berengaria. By 1221 there was only one royal *bailliage* left in the whole of Greater Anjou, the *bailliage* of Tours. In

Poitou it was a similar story (see p. 104). By 1238 the real masters of Poitou were the Lusignans. They held no fewer than 21 castellanies; and the combined total held by the houses of Lusignan, Thouars and Mauleon was 36. By this date the crown held only four. In 1199, by contrast, Richard had held 13 castellanies in Poitou and even in 1202–3 John still had 12 (including those he held in his wife's right). While it is true that the four still controlled in 1238 included both Poitiers and La Rochelle, it is likely that La Rochelle at least had been worth more a generation earlier.

The fact is that whereas in Normandy Philip had more or less stepped straight into John's shoes, in Anjou and Poitou nothing of the kind happened. Dramatic political changes beginning in 1199 mean that it is impossible to use the accounts of 1221 and 1238 as any sort of indication of the level of Angevin revenues from those two provinces in the 1180s and 1190s. If we based estimates of English revenues in the 1180s and 1190s on figures taken from the early pipe rolls of Henry III's reign, we might think income was less than £10,000 a year, when we know it was in fact two or three times as much. In these circumstances we have no option but to bear in mind the prosperity and commercial importance of these regions and guess accordingly.

Whatever rough guess we choose to make, it must be certain that at the start of his reign John was significantly richer than Philip. While it is true that Philip's territorial acquisitions in the north east, notably around Amiens and Arras, meant that by the early 1190s he was wealthier than his father had been after 1152, this is far from proving that he was already as well off as the Angevins. By 1200 though Philip had won the Evrécin, he had relinquished Aire and St Omer to the count of Flanders. Indeed, the anonymous chronicler of Béthune – a man well placed to know the value of Philip's north-eastern gains and losses – believed that there was an obvious explanation for Philip's setbacks in the wars of 1194–8; 'because in terms of land and money King Richard was richer than the king of France'.

Or is it possible that this observer was deceived? Did Richard only look richer because he was taxing his subjects so hard – so hard that within a few years he would have found himself left high and dry as the helpless ruler of exhausted lands? Is this the legacy bequeathed to John? It has often been argued that the Norman Exchequer Rolls of 1195 and 1198 reveal a duchy squeezed to the limit. If Richard had indeed outspent Philip, was it John who had to pay the price? The exchequer roll for 1200–1 shows that John was still able to levy tallages in Normandy, but as evidence is too fragmentary to bear much weight. Two points, however, should be remembered. First, that virtually all of the Norman revenue raised to pay for the war was spent in Normandy itself. Second, that whereas the destruction of war in 1193–99 was chiefly confined to the Vexin and the north-east frontier of Normandy, expenditure – including the expenditure of money drawn from elsewhere, in particular from England – was more widely diffused throughout the duchy. Hence it may well be that, as Powicke argued long ago, 'Normandy as a whole was prob-ably not impoverished and did not feel the strain which was put upon England by the constant exportation of men and treasure'.[4] If not Normandy, then had England been impoverished by Richard's unrelenting demands for money throughout the 1190s?

Grumbling comments made by Roger of Howden and William of Newburgh show that towards the end of the reign many people in England felt financially oppressed. According to Ralph of Coggeshall, 'no age can remember, no history can record any preced-ing king who exacted so much money from his kingdom as that king amassed in the five years after he returned from captivity'. But whether or not the country had been impoverished is another ques-tion altogether. Our answer to this question will depend above all else on the level of revenues that John was able to raise in England in early years of his reign (1199–1203). In fact, he continued to raise sums from England just as great as those which Richard had been taking in the last years of his reign. If we assign the financial year 1199 to both kings, we find that Richard's revenue in the last five years of his reign (1195–99) averaged about £24,500, whereas John's revenues in the five-year period 1199–1203 – the years most relevant to the disasters he suffered on the continent – averaged over £27,000. (This average includes a rather low estimate, just £15,000, of the yield from the Seventh of 1203 – though the Thirteenth of 1207 is recorded as producing £57,421, and a high estimate for the Seventh would add substantially to John's income.) Although the relatively high rate of inflation between 1198 and 1204 may mean that £27,000 for John was worth no more than £24,500 for Richard, these figures lend no support whatsoever to the notion that England in 1200 was more impoverished than in 1194.[5] Indeed, of course, in

---

4 F. M. Powicke, *The Loss of Normandy* (Manchester, 2nd edn., 1960), p. 239.

5 Most recent studies of prices in the light of economic conditions and John's fiscal demands tend to limit the period of significant inflation to 1198 and 1204, and see it as followed by a period of price stability, if not indeed, deflation. J. L. Bolton, 'The English Economy in the early thirteenth century', and P. Latimer, 'Early thirteenth-century prices', both in S. Church, *King John: New Interpretations* (Woodbridge, 1999).

the middle years of John's reign royal revenue to England was to climb at an astonishing rate (pp. 58, 103). All in all there can be no doubt that *c*.1200 the overall resources of the Angevin Empire were a good deal greater than those at the disposal of Philip Augustus.

But this is a very different matter from saying that John actually spent more on the war in Normandy than Philip did. The most recent attempt to compare the revenues of the two kings in 1202–3 has concluded that although by then overall Capetian revenues had not outstripped those of the Angevins, Philip may have enjoyed an advantage in terms of the amount of cash available for military operations on the Norman frontier during the summer of 1203.[6] In other words, Philip had been able to concentrate his financial resources in a critical theatre of war more effectively than John had. It was not just a question of resources but also of the way the resources were used. In explaining what happened in 1202–4, it is not the developments of the 1190s that are decisive but the actions of the kings in 1201 and afterwards. John's problem was that he was unable to mobilize the huge resources of his empire and bring them to bear in the armed struggle against Philip Augustus. Why was this? Was it because the Angevin Empire was a cumbersome political structure, administratively incoherent and over-extended when compared with the more compact Capetian kingdom? But if this were so, then how do we explain Richard's success in war against the same opponent in the years 1194 to 1198?

The root of John's problems lay not in any underlying structural weaknesses but in the realms of policy and diplomacy. By 1202 he had driven all the most powerful nobles of Poitou and Anjou to revolt. Richard too had had rebels to face – but in the Limousin and Angoumois, regions where ducal authority had always been weak. It was John's particular talent to conjure up revolt right in the heartland of the empire. In Anjou and Poitou John and his commanders found themselves on the defensive; the rebels did Philip's fighting for him. In some cases they did not even have to fight in order to capture John's expensively maintained strongholds. In 1203 Beaufort and Châteauneuf-sur-Sarthe were simply handed over; their defenders knew they would get no help from John.

---

6 N. Barratt, 'The revenues of John and Philip Augustus revisited', in S. Church (ed.), *King John: New Interpretations* (Woodbridge, 1999), p. 84. However, Barratt also argues that Philip had to pay more for his soldiers and that, 'in real terms, it is likely that any financial superiority he might have enjoyed would have been negated. The causes for the loss of Normandy in 1204 must therefore be sought elsewhere'.

In Gascony too John was on the defensive. The key to Richard's strategy here had been first the alliance with Sancho of Navarre, then – when the king of Navarre became an unreliable ally, immersed in a losing war against Castile – an alliance with Raymond VI of Toulouse. But by the end of 1202 Count Raymond had switched sides and was in the Capetian camp. Moreover, Philip Augustus had already won for himself a new and, from John's point of view, a particularly dangerous ally: Alfonso VIII of Castile – dangerous partly because he had a good claim to Gascony. John's only friend in the south, Sancho VII of Navarre, was precisely the prince who was least likely to be able to help him in the coming struggle. Philip had no need to consider what might happen if Navarrese troops were to march into the Touraine – as they had done, on Richard's behalf, in 1194. By 1202 whatever resources John had in the south were pinned down in the south.

It was the same story in the north east. As Richard's ally, Count Baldwin IX of Flanders had defeated Philip in 1197 and had captured St-Omer in 1198. Another of Richard's allies, Renaud count of Boulogne had, according to Philip's biographer, Rigord of St-Denis, 'inflicted great damage on the French kingdom'. In the late 1190s, in other words, Philip had been forced to fight on more than one front (see p. 49). But by 1202 the boot was on the other foot. Although John began to renew contacts with Otto IV in April and a treaty was made in September 1202, Otto's first priority was naturally his struggle with his rival for the German throne, Philip of Swabia, and not until the summer of 1203 did he consider his position strong enough to allow him to begin to talk about a campaign in support of his uncle. By then it was too late. In any case only in alliance with the count of Flanders was German military intervention a realistic prospect. But Baldwin's departure on crusade meant that Flanders had been neutralized. As for Renaud of Boulogne, he was now in the Capetian camp; in 1201 Philip had betrothed his son Philip Hurepel – of doubtful legitimacy but a king's son for all that – to Renaud's heiress daughter. During the conquest of Normandy Renaud was to be one of Philip's most distinguished commanders. Politically and diplomatically Philip had outmanoeuvred John. John had to dissipate his resources, in Gascony, in the Loire valley, on the Norman frontier; Philip could concentrate his where and when he chose. The fact that in these unfavourable circumstances John could afford to spend as much as he did on the defence of Normandy only serves to strengthen the overall impression of great Angevin wealth, in particular in this case the wealth of England and Ireland – the only provinces where

John's position was as yet unchallenged and, from which therefore, he could afford to send reserves of cash. (In 1215–16 when it was England which was under threat we find the flow of men and money moving in the opposite direction: from Poitou to England.)

Yet despite the barrel-loads of silver which were sent across the Channel in 1202–3 Normandy was lost – and lost swiftly. Contemporary English chroniclers were concerned to explain the loss; it mattered to them in a way that the loss of Anjou and the imminent loss of Poitou and Gascony did not. They were unanimous in ascribing it not to John's inadequate resources but to a lack of trust between king and those of his subjects who were born, like him, to wealth and power. John was treacherous and he feared treachery. Recent events in Anjou and Poitou had served only to confirm his fears. His response was to rely more and more on professional soldiers – men like Brandin, Martin Algais, Gerard d'Athée and Louvrecaire, all of whom he appointed to high office in 1202 and 1203. Later letters and government inquiries show that people in Normandy long remembered the depredations of the mercenary bands who were supposed to be protecting them. 'Why', asked the biographer of William Marshal, 'was John unable to keep the love of his people? It was because Louvrecaire maltreated them and pillaged them as though he were in an enemy's country.' William Marshal spent the whole of 1202 and 1203 actively engaged in the defence of Normandy. His biography was based on the memories, or memoirs, of his squire, John of Earley, who was in his master's service throughout the critical period. As evidence for well-informed aristocratic opinion *L'Histoire de Guillaume le Maréchal* could hardly be bettered. It presents us with a picture – amply confirmed from other sources, record sources as well as narratives – of an obsessively suspicious king:

> When he left Rouen he had his baggage sent on ahead secretly and silently. At Bonneville he stayed the night in the castle, not in the town, for he feared a trap, believing that his barons had sworn to hand him over to the king of France . . . in the morning he slipped away before daybreak while everyone thought he was still asleep.[7]

Who could feel confidence in such a king or wish to fight for him? He was believed to be capable of murdering his nephew but not of organizing the defence of a beleaguered province. On that belief he foundered.

---

7 *Histoire de Guillaume le Maréchal*, (ed.) P. Meyer, 3 vols (Paris, 1891–1901), vol. 2, pp. 96–7.

# 8 The end of the empire

## THE FAILURE OF GRAND STRATEGY, 1214

After the holding operation of 1206, eight years were to go by before John's next visit to the Continent. In what was to become a familiar thirteenth-century pattern, withdrawal from France was followed by renewed military activity in the British Isles. An attack on Braose country in South Wales in 1208, an armed demonstration on the Scottish border in 1209, an expedition against the Lacys in Ireland in 1210, two campaigns against Llywelyn ap Iorwerth in North Wales in 1211, all meant that, in the view of the Barnwell annalist, John managed to achieve a greater preponderance in Ireland, Scotland and Wales than any of his predecessors. In Normandy the annalist of Jumièges even heard that John had more than made up for his losses there by what he had gained in Wales and Ireland. What is certain is that John was now extremely rich. A quarrel with the church had led to him confiscating church property throughout England; profits were so great that rather than seek to end the interdict that Pope Innocent III imposed in 1208, he preferred being excommunicated. Taxes on the Jews brought in large sums and he was systematically driving up routine sources of income collected by sheriffs and from barons. Whereas in the early part of his reign revenues audited at the Exchequer (i.e. excluding interdict and Jewish revenues) only once – in 1205 – exceeded £30,000, the equivalent figures for 1210, 1211 and 1212 are £51,913, £83,291 and £56,612. It has been estimated that by 1212 he had the astonishing sum of 200,000 marks in coin stored in castle treasuries at Bristol, Gloucester, Corfe and elsewhere.

By 1212 John was ready to return to the Continent but the expedition planned for Poitou had first to be redirected to meet the threat of rebellion in Wales then cancelled when he received news of a baronial conspiracy in England. Philip Augustus once again made preparations to invade England but on 30 May 1213 the earl of Salisbury attacked and destroyed the French invasion fleet as it lay at anchor at Damme. Jubilant at this success John ordered the force he had mustered for the defence of England to sail at once to Poitou. As in 1205 the magnates refused to go with him. Some northern barons claimed that the terms of their tenure did not require them to serve in Poitou. Indeed, the English political situation was still far from being settled when John eventually decided to press on regardless. In February 1214 he landed at La Rochelle. Having gone to the trouble and expense of building up a confederation of allies headed by the emperor, Otto IV, and the counts of Flanders and Boulogne – precisely the alliances that he had sacrificed in 1200 – John was probably right to strike while the iron was hot. He had learned the lesson of 1202–4 and had adopted a strategy which would force Philip to divide his forces. While his allies kept the Capetian busy in the north east, he himself would launch an attack in the west. It was a policy which had worked well in the last few years of Richard's reign. John, though, was taking a risk. Failure abroad could only lead to a deepening of the crisis in England. Moreover the problems awaiting John in south-west France were very considerable ones. On Gascony's eastern frontier a new and aggressive force had arrived in the shape of the Albigensian Crusade led by Simon de Montfort. In a series of attacks on the lands of Raymond VI of Toulouse Simon had been deterred neither by John's feeble attempts to help his brother-in-law nor by any qualms about Angevin rights over Quercy and the Agenais. In 1212 Simon hanged Martin Algais, once John's seneschal of Gascony. In the same year his capture of Marmande brought him to within a few miles of La Réole, a key Angevin fortress on the Garonne. During the course of his 1214 expedition John spent a few days in Gascony and made a perfunctory bid to assert his rights in the Agenais, but when Simon ejected John's garrisons and then resumed his advance into Perigord he was able to do so without hindrance. John's main concern was with Poitou and the old Angevin lands to the north.

As Table 8.1 indicates, Poitou at the end of John's reign was very different from the Poitou of its beginning.[1] Whereas between 1152 and 1199 the number of castellanies held by the three most powerful Poitevin families remained fairly constant, after 1199 the number rose sharply. The real watershed here was the Lusignan revolt of 1201–4. Thereafter John's authority was confined to the south west

---

1  Table 8.1 based on the appendix to R. Hajdu, 'Castles, castellans and the structure of politics in Poitou, 1152–1271', *Journal of Medieval History*, 4 (1978).

**Table 8.1** Number of castellanies held in Poiton

|  | 1152 | 1172 | 1189 | 1199 | 1206 | 1216 |
|---|---|---|---|---|---|---|
| Number of castellanies held by count of Poitou | 10 | 10 | 15 | 13 | 12* | 9* |
| Number held by houses of Lusignan, Mauléon and Thouars | 18 | 16 | 16 | 18 | 27 | 36 |

* including 5 (4 in 1216) held as the inheritance of Isabella of Angoulême.

of the province, to the county of Angoulême, to Saintonge and to Aunis (La Rochelle, Niort and St Jean d'Angély). The rest of Poitou acknowledged Philip, yet Philip had never invaded Poitou as he had Normandy. All that had happened was that the most powerful lords of Poitou had offered their allegiance to Philip and he, in return, had made them more powerful still. In 1204, for example, he appointed Aimeri of Thouars hereditary seneschal of Poitou. This was an easy and inexpensive way for Philip to extend his rule, but inevitably it meant that his authority tended to be notional rather than real. The king of France very rarely visited his new province and never went beyond Poitiers. He even offered to hand over the whole comital domain in Poitou to Ralph of Lusignan for five years on the grounds that the land was too remote for him to go there himself or to retain effective control over his officials. This abdication of crown rights in Poitou was not negligence; it was conscious policy. From 1204 onwards Philip's one great concern was to ensure that he kept Normandy; to a king of Paris control of the lower Seine Valley was crucial. Compared with this overriding priority, everything else came a poor second. In 1206, for example, Philip had been at Nantes when he heard that John was preparing to sail. At once he moved north east to supervise the defence of Normandy, allowing John to disembark unchallenged at La Rochelle. Philip was always more interested in invading England than in completing his take-over of the continental lands of the Angevins. This was because the threat to Normandy came from England not from south-west France.

In these circumstances, with two rival kings both claiming to be lord of Poitou, but neither prepared to spend time there or give it a high priority, there were bound to be profound changes in the province's political structure. It became a land dominated by a small group of regional lords: the Lusignan, Mauléon and Thouars families. The best that a king could do was to enter into a game of diplomacy with these *de facto* independent powers. Thus in 1214 John could arrive with any army and put military pressure on the Lusignans. In a report sent back to England he wrote triumphantly of his success in bringing them to submit. What this actually meant was that he arranged a betrothal between his daughter Joan and Hugh of Lusignan's son, also called Hugh, and granted them Saintes, Saintonge and Oléron until some more permanent provision in Anjou and Touraine could be arranged. Some submission! In reality the Lusignans had been persuaded to change sides and had exacted a high price in return, including custody of Joan.

By the end of May 1214 John had obtained the allegiance of the Limousin and had all three of the great Poitevin houses on his side. He was now confident enough to go over to the attack. First he threatened Nantes, presumably hoping to win over the new duke of Brittany, King Philip's cousin, Peter of Dreux, by the same combination of carrot and stick that had proved effective with the Lusignans. Peter of Dreux's claim to the duchy was based on his marriage to Alice, daughter of Constance and Guy of Thouars. But Eleanor of Brittany, the sister of the murdered Arthur, clearly had a better right than Alice, and John – who had captured her at Mirebeau – had brought her with him. Thus John was in a position both to tempt Peter by offering him the rich honour of Richmond, the traditional English holding of the duke of Brittany, and to threaten him with the presence of Eleanor. In the event, not even the capture of his brother Robert in a skirmish near Nantes persuaded Peter of Dreux to join John's coalition, though it may have led him to agree not to interfere with John's subsequent military manoeuvres. Moving up the Loire John entered Angers, unopposed, on 17 June. Two days later he laid siege to Roche-au-Moine, a newly-built castle belonging to William des Roches. But when Prince Louis of France brought an army from Chinon to relieve Roche-au-Moine (2 July) John was unable to persuade the Poitevins to fight. Feeling himself left in the lurch, he beat a hasty retreat.

Even more disastrous for John was the defeat of his Rhineland allies at the Battle of Bouvines (27 July 1214). Roche-au-Moine had been a blow to morale but John could at least claim that by keeping his army intact he had salvaged the strategy of compelling Philip Augustus to divide his forces. After Bouvines, however, Philip was free to join his son in the west. In these circumstances John could not expect to retain the allegiance of the Poitevin lords and it was only Philip's relative lack of interest in this part of the world that made him listen to John's overtures. On 18 September the two kings agreed to a five years' truce. In mid-October 1214 John arrived back in England. After eight months of effort his continental territories were in no better shape than on the day he disembarked at La Rochelle and in England a storm was brewing. By taking so much coin out of circulation in pursuit of his foreign policy objectives he had made it hard for his subjects to meet his fiscal demands. In the Barnwell chronicler's opinion he had became the plunderer of his subjects. He was now a failed plunderer.

## THE CAPETIAN INVASION OF ENGLAND, 1215–17

Less than two years after his withdrawal from Roche-au-Moine John was once more to be found on the retreat before Prince Louis of France. This time it was on the beaches of England that John chose not to fight. With commendable efficiency and foresight he had mustered his army in the right place and at the right time but, when he saw Louis's troops disembarking at Sandwich on 22 May 1216, the comforts of his chambers at Winchester suddenly seemed irresistible.

In timing his descent upon England Louis had, of course, taken advantage of the turmoil associated with the movement to obtain and implement Magna Carta. In the autumn of 1215 the rebel barons, realizing that John had no intention of keeping his promise to observe the terms of the charter, sent a request for help to the Capetian court and offered the crown to Prince Louis. Rebels normally looked to a discontented member of the ruling family to supply leadership or, at least, a figurehead for revolt. With John's own sons both too young and too firmly under their father's control to be available, Louis of France was the most obvious candidate. (If John had died without children, Louis, husband of Henry II's granddaughter Blanche of Castile, might well have inherited all the Plantagenet lands.) Louis accepted the offer and in November 1215 sent a contingent of knights to reinforce the rebel garrison of London. In the following May he launched a full-scale invasion.

After John's ignominious retreat from the Kent coast his position crumbled rapidly. Louis entered London and then captured Winchester. In August King Alexander of Scotland came to Canterbury to do homage to a Capetian king of England. By this time Louis already controlled most of the eastern counties except for the castles of Dover, Windsor and Lincoln. Had he succeeded, then a Capetian conquest of England would have followed upon the earlier Norman and Angevin conquests, each conquest resulting in the creation of an ever larger French empire. But during the night of 18–19 October 1216, with the outcome of the war still in doubt, John died. He had inspired neither affection nor loyalty and once he had shown that, no matter how hard he tried, he lacked Richard's ability to command victory in war, then he was lost. 'No man may ever trust him', wrote Bertrand de Born, 'for his heart is soft and cowardly'. Not even the Angevin governmental machine could sustain him against that damning verdict.

From Louis's point of view John's death was a disaster. Even a child king presented a more formidable opponent than John had done, particularly when that child's council included several elder statesmen and a papal legate capable of turning a dynastic struggle into a holy war. More important still was the fact that prevailing sentiment disliked the idea of depriving a boy of his inheritance; now that the father was dead there was no need to go through with so uncomfortable a scheme. With John out of the way, there was nothing to stop the regency council reissuing Magna Carta, a measure which had the effect of depriving Louis of a major part of his platform. Finding English support ebbing away from him, Louis was compelled to rely more and more on fellow Frenchmen and on reinforcements from abroad: this only made him more unpopular still. After his forces had been defeated both on land (Lincoln, May 1217) and at sea (Sandwich, August 1217), he had little choice but to come to terms (the Treaty of Lambeth, September 1217), and withdraw. It was not in the text of the treaty but widely believed in England, that Louis promised he would try to persuade his father to restore the lost Angevin dominions.

## GOVERNMENT WITHOUT CASH: THE MINORITY OF HENRY III

In time of war, when policy objectives were relatively clear, a child king made an adequate figurehead, but with the restoration of peace came complications that required mature and undisputed political leadership. But how could there be undisputed leadership now? Which – if any – of the king's counsellors had a better claim than his fellows and rivals to control the king and 'his' crown? Who could say? Moreover, the urgent need to win support during the wars of

1215–17 had meant that many royal assets had been given away; to those local magnates such as Falkes de Bréauté who had won the war for Henry III it seemed right that they should now be allowed to enjoy the fruits of their loyalty. In this situation royal power quietly disintegrated. In Ireland the justiciar Geoffrey de Marisco went his own way. In Wales the position was even worse. Llywelyn ap Iorwerth 'the Great' of Gwynedd, Prince of North Wales, had brilliantly exploited both civil war and weak government to obtain a dominating position in south as well as in north Wales. He now held the old English royal centres of Cardigan and Carmarthen, and in 1220 he humiliated the most powerful English lord of south Wales, William Marshal's son, the new earl of Pembroke. In England itself the capacity of men who were lords of castles and sheriffdoms to keep the profits of government for themselves ensured that royal revenue in the three years 1218–20 averaged only £8,000 a year – a fraction of the amount that had been collected annually for the past 60 years. So penniless a king as young Henry III was in no position to influence events in western France.

In these years there were many who believed that Louis, disappointed of England, was likely to renew the attack on Aquitaine. In 1219, on his way to join the crusade against the Albigensian heretics and their protector, Raymond VI of Toulouse, he passed through the Limousin and this, together with his contribution to the sack of Marmande (June 1219), set the alarm bells ringing. Fortunately for the impoverished minority government and its hapless representatives in Aquitaine it turned out to be a false alarm. Philip Augustus was, as ever, basically uninterested in the south west; in 1220 he agreed to renew the truce with the Plantagenets for four more years. Not until after the old king's death was a further Capetian advance likely.

By this date the political transformation of Poitou had gone a stage further still. John's widow, Isabella of Angoulême, had returned home in 1218. She had quickly become convinced that a part of her patrimony was being withheld and, in consequence, relations between her and the minority government in England became strained. In 1220 she married again. For the second time in twenty years the marriage of Isabella of Angoulême was to have major political consequences. This time she chose her own husband: Hugh of Lusignan, count of La Marche, her daughter Joan's fiancé and son of the Hugh to whom she had herself been betrothed before John carried her off twenty years earlier. Although he had not married

Joan, Hugh of Lusignan had managed to retain possession of her and her intended dowry, Saintes and Oléron. But the minority government had neither a realistic chance of giving him lands in Anjou and Touraine (as envisaged in 1214), nor any intention of granting him Saintes and Oléron in perpetuity. It could not even afford to keep up payment of fees to Hugh's knights, so it was hardly surprising that he began to think he could do better by transferring his allegiance. Thus when Isabella married Hugh she claimed she was acting in her son's interest. Hugh, she pointed out, might have married a Capetian bride and had he done so 'all your land in Poitou and Gascony, and our land too, would have been lost'. So weak was the position of the seneschal by 1219–20 that it was a plausible argument. But it meant that from now on everything depended on what Hugh did. As Isabella's husband, count of Angoulême as well as of La Marche, he became the undisputed arbiter of politics in this part of the world. He now demanded not only her dower lands in England, but also Merpins and Niort, and exerted military pressure to get them. Since a penniless government was unable to send out from England a seneschal equipped with the resources to restore ducal authority in Aquitaine – as the towns wanted (p. 64) – it resorted in 1221 to the expedient of appointing the second most powerful noble, Savari de Mauléon, lord of Talmont, in the hope that he might be able to stand up to Hugh. But even he could do no more than obtain a truce.

## THE LOSS OF LA ROCHELLE

When the news of the death of Philip Augustus (14 July 1223) arrived in England, the justiciar Hubert de Burgh ordered the muster of a fleet and army at Portsmouth, and sent envoys to France to demand that Louis VIII's coronation be delayed until he had restored Normandy, as he – allegedly – had promised in 1217. At the same time Hubert offered to grant Hugh and Isabella much of what they demanded, the plan being to put an end to discord in Poitou so as to be able to concentrate on the recovery of Normandy. Henry III's ministers were in an optimistic frame of mind, and with some reason. Over the last two years the English government had begun to pull itself out of the morass into which civil war had plunged it. It had successfully resumed control of a number of castles and sheriff-doms. By Michaelmas 1222 royal revenue had climbed to about £12,500, and would reach nearly £14,000 in 1223. The earl of

Pembroke had defeated Llywelyn and recovered Cardigan and Carmarthen for the crown. It looked as though at last things were under control.

The envoys sent to France arrived too late, however, and Louis treated their message with contempt, threatening a new invasion of England if further hostile moves were made. In these circumstances the government very sensibly decided to back down and ask for a four-year prolongation of the truce that was due to expire at Easter 1224. Louis then surprised them by suggesting that the truce should be extended by ten years. In January 1224 he had agreed to Pope Honorius III's request that he go once again to fight the church's fight against the heretics of Toulouse, and he wanted to be sure that Henry III would not intervene on the side of his cousin (Raymond VII). While considering this, the government completed negotiations with Hugh de Lusignan, granting him possession of Saintes and Oléron for four years, and 200 marks p.a. in lieu of Niort. Although the truce expired on 14 April, Hubert took its imminent renewal for granted and still remained confident. Prospects in Wales and Ireland looked good, and he was determined to bring Falkes de Bréauté to heel. He was caught totally off-guard when on 5 May, the day fixed for the beginning of Louis's crusade, the king of France announced that he would not, after all, renew the truce. Just a few days earlier he had received a new message from the pope, postponing the crusade on the grounds that Raymond VII of Toulouse was ready to submit to the church. Exasperated and with an army ready to go, he decided to march into Poitou instead. Despite the fact that the English government had urged Pope Honorius to come to a settlement with Raymond, it had failed to anticipate this outcome. In haste it took steps to defend Poitou. On 26 May a former seneschal of Aquitaine, Geoffrey de Neville, was despatched to La Rochelle with 2,000 marks and Hugh of Lusignan was sent the 1,400 marks he was owed. Galleys were despatched from Bayonne to help with the defence of La Rochelle and Niort.

But on 2 June Hubert received an even greater shock. In May Hugh of Lusignan and Louis VIII had met at Bourges and there Louis made Hugh 'an offer which he could not refuse'. Louis offered Saintes and Oléron in hereditary right, and 2,000 *l.p.* a year to compensate him for loss of Isabella's dower lands in England until he had lands of equivalent value in conquered Poitou. He also promised him Langeais or, if it could be taken, Bordeaux! Only a government not much interested in western France could have made such an offer, and no thirteenth-century English government could possibly have matched it. So Louis and Hugh sealed the treaty which settled the fate of La Rochelle, Niort and St Jean d'Angély. The English government called a council meeting at Northampton for 16 June, probably intending to seek approval for a tax to raise the large sum that would be needed to defend Poitou. In the meantime, however, it sent no more cash to La Rochelle and pressed on with measures against Falkes. When Falkes resisted, the Northampton meeting was adjourned to lay siege to Bedford Castle on 19 June. The garrison commanded by Falkes's brother William held out for eight weeks, eventually surrendering on 14 August. By this time La Rochelle had fallen. Hubert de Burgh had probably failed to anticipate that Falkes would be prepared to take up arms in defence of his rights, and had certainly failed to anticipate that William de Bréauté would put up such a stubborn resistance. Not until 19 July, when it was too late, were further funds despatched to La Rochelle. The priorities of June and July 1224 revealed just how much had changed – but the priorities of 1224 were criticized by the pope at the time and by Henry III himself years later.

Louis's invasion of Poitou turned into a triumphal procession. From Tours he went to Montreuil-Bellay and and granted pensions for the viscount of Thouars. Niort capitulated on 5 July, two days after Louis's arrival outside the town. Elsewhere, the viscount of Limoges decided that the moment had come to offer his submission to the French crown. Louis VIII entered St Jean d'Angély unopposed and then, on 15 July, drew up his army outside the walls of the last Angevin bastion in Poitou. It became clear that the English government was much more interested in the siege of Bedford than in the siege of La Rochelle. 'To the citizens of La Rochelle it must have seemed that the English government had taken leave of its senses'.[2] In these circumstances, as at Rouen in 1204, prolonged resistance seemed pointless and on 3 August 1224 the city surrendered. Henry III's government could not afford to ignore what Falkes and William de Bréauté were doing, but with them the day of reckoning could have been postponed. So far as the much greater threat posed by Louis VIII's invasion was concerned, they had to act now or never. If the government had pessimistically decided that the fall of La Rochelle was inevitable, that would have been one thing – and perfectly rational too in view of Hugh of Lusignan's change of allegiance and the

2  D. A. Carpenter, *The Minority of Henry III* (London, 1990), p. 372.

underlying financial strength of the Capetian monarchy after its conquest of Normandy (see below p. 114). But as it happened, La Rochelle fell not as a consequence of a realistic acceptance of the inevitable, but as the product of too much optimism. For too long Hubert had continued to imagine he could deal with a number of different problems simultaneously. As early as 1220 Pandulf, the papal legate to England and a shrewd observer, had chided him, and in the context of Poitevin business, for the confidence with which he bestrode seas and mountains, trying to attain the unattainable.

In retrospect we can see that the fall of La Rochelle marked the end of the Angevin Empire. While John still held La Rochelle he had a fortified landing place from which he could attempt, as in 1206 and 1214, to regain Poitou and Anjou. Subsequent attempts had to disembark at much less convenient ports: St Malo in 1230 and Royan in 1242. From this point on, until the mid-fourteenth century, of the former continental dominions, only Gascony remained in Plantagenet hands. This was not, of course, at all clear to contemporaries. So far as Louis VIII was concerned, Gascony was within the kingdom of France and although he returned to Paris in September, there was no reason to call a halt to the campaign of conquest. The treaty he had made at Bourges had envisaged Hugh of Lusignan as lord of Bordeaux and so, during the autumn and winter of 1224, Count Hugh, in command of Louis's army, set about the conquest of Gascony. In swift succession St Emilion, St Macaire, Langon, La Réole and Bazas opened their gates to his officers. Some Gascon lords too offered him their allegiance. Yet, as in 1205–6, Bordeaux and Bayonne held out – and as La Rochelle could have done in 1224. Moreover the loss of La Rochelle had stung the English government and political community into belated action. The king's younger brother, Richard of Cornwall, was given the title 'count of Poitou' and sent out as an indication of the government's resolve. The yield of the Fifteenth of 1225, about £40,000, showed what resources were available if a political consensus could be obtained; about £35,000 of this was spent on purposes related to the recovery and defence of Gascony. This show of strength in 1225, so signally lacking in 1224, was sufficient to turn the tide. By November 1225 La Réole, the last of the Capetian-held fortresses in Gascony, had reverted to its old allegiance.

The English government was still not prepared to accept the loss of the Plantagenet lands. In 1230 Henry III marched from Brittany to Bordeaux and did at least manage to recover the isle of Oléron.

But the main lesson of the 1230 expedition was that while Hugh of Lusignan remained loyal to the Capetian cause there was no hope of making any real headway in Poitou. For this reason English hopes were raised when Louis IX's brother, Alphonse, was invested as count of Poitou in 1241. For Isabella of Angoulême after twenty years of queening it over Poitou this was more than she could bear. She persuaded her husband to defy Louis IX and encouraged her son to try again. Henry III landed at Royan in May 1242 but he was no general. In the Taillebourg campaign he was outmanoeuvred by Louis IX. By August Hugh of Lusignan was forced to admit that he had miscalculated badly. He swallowed his pride – and Isabella's – and submitted to Louis on humiliating terms. The campaign of 1242 marked the end of Henry III's attempts to recover his lands by force. Thereafter when he visited France he went in peace, full of admiration for what he saw.

How are we to explain Henry's failure to recover his ancestral dominions? Personalities certainly came into it for the pious and powerful French king was everything that Henry III would have liked to have been, but it was also a question of resources. Philip's conquest of Normandy had made an enormous difference to the balance of power and, since the Bibliothèque Nationale's recent acquisition of a Capetian financial account for 1221, a measurable difference. This shows that the ordinary annual income of the French crown now stood at about 200,000 *l.p.* (roughly £65,000), almost twice what it had been on the eve of the territorial gains of 1203–4. It shows moreover that Philip had started the year with a balance in hand of 132,000 *l.p.* (over £43,000) and that his expenses were running at only about two-thirds of his income. The French king, in other words, was now very comfortably off and apparently getting richer every year. Next year, when he drew up his testament, Philip felt able to make bequests totalling nearly 800,000 *l.p.* (£250,000)!

The wealth and power of the French crown were vividly demonstrated in the crisis which followed the sudden death of Louis VIII in November 1226, leaving a 12-year-old boy as his heir. This was an event which, in Denholm-Young's words, 'set all the political weathercocks spinning'.[3] The English government took the opportunity to try to lure Hugh and Isabella back into the fold but the inducements they had to offer were simply insufficient. The French regent, Blanche of Castile, was easily able to outbid them. Once Louis IX

---

3  N. Denholm-Young, *Richard of Cornwall* (Oxford, 1947), p. 7.

had grown up enough to be master in his own house, then the balance of power tipped even further. Neither in resources nor in character was Henry III any match for Saint Louis. The verdicts of 1203–4 and 1224 were indeed irreversible. Only with the greatest reluctance was Henry III brought to recognize this state of affairs. He still, on occasions, felt himself to be an Angevin. In 1254 he visited Fontevraud, rearranged the tombs of his ancestors, and asked that his own heart should be buried there (as it was). But dynastic sentiment was one thing; the realities of power another. To challenge the crown of France was to run the risk of losing Gascony as well. In the Capetian view Gascony was one of the territories forfeited by King John in 1202 and the events of 1294–95 were to show just how difficult it would be to defend it against a sudden attack. In these circumstances the terms of the treaty of Paris (1259) were generous. Henry gave up his claims to Normandy, Anjou and Poitou; in return Louis IX accepted his homage for Gascony. The settlement of 1259 completed the 'great transformation' (see p. 1). From now on Gascony remained a subordinate province inalienably attached to an English monarchy.

By the end of his reign Henry III was indisputably an English king and men were beginning to think of the Plantagenets as an English dynasty. A French poet of the period took it for granted that Richard the Lionheart had been buried in London. This way of re-modelling the past to fit the facts of the late thirteenth-century present has proved to be astonishingly long-lived. Even today English historians are still a little inclined to write as though Henry II and his sons were first and foremost kings of England, whose primary duty was to stay in England and look after their 'real subjects'.

# 9 Conclusion

The Angevin Empire was a family firm. It existed for the benefit of the family. The interests of the family counted for more than any notion of keeping the empire intact under a single ruler. Even though there are signs of a movement towards legal and administrative uniformity (pp. 80–82), this was the result of drift, of *ad hoc* responses to particular problems, rather than of consciously centralising intention. Henry II and his sons treated their various French territories no differently from the way Philip Augustus and Louis VIII dealt with the various French provinces which they acquired. Neither the Angevins nor the Capetians set out to establish a centralized state – it would have been counter-productive had they tried, and anachronistic to imagine that they might have tried. As things turned out, Henry II's union of three distinct blocs (Anglo-Norman, Angevin and Aquitanian) survived intact for only 50 years (1154–1204), and this meant that, with one important exception, there had not been time for the people who lived in the different parts to develop those routine patterns of thought and action that might have created a political, economic and cultural community of interests strong enough to prevent the ruling dynasty from dividing their empire up again whenever it suited them to do so. The one exception was the growing importance of commercial ties between on the one hand, England and Ireland, and on the other, the ports of western France where by the early thirteenth century sterling coin was beginning to circulate. This economic interest was strong enough to create in those towns an active political will in favour of retaining the 'imperial connection'. In the case of the Gascon towns, above all Bordeaux and Bayonne, this was sufficient to ensure the survival of 'English' Gascony for another 250 years. In the case of La Rochelle and Niort, the same combination of commercial interest and political will turned out to be insufficient, in the particular circumstances of the early 1220s, to withstand the immediate pressure of Capetian and Lusignan military power. Similarly, the longer-established and much wider community of interests between

Normandy and England had been insufficient in the political circumstances of 1202–4 to withstand the immediate military pressure of Philip Augustus's invasion.

## A PLANTAGENET CULTURE? HISTORY, MYTH AND ARCHITECTURE

Not surprisingly contemporary narratives give very little sense of the Angevin Empire as a family firm with a historical culture which embraced all its branches. Where the writing of dynastic history was still practised – as it was not in Aquitaine – its strength was regional rather than 'imperial'. There were a few straws in the wind. In Anjou itself the early twelfth-century *Gesta Consulum Andegavorum (Deeds of the counts of Anjou)* was continued as far as 1151 by John of Marmoutier, dedicated to Henry II and given a new prologue taken from Bede – an 'appropriate blending of Henry IIs traditional Angevin and new English cultural backgrounds'.[1] An author from the Touraine, Benoît de Sainte-Maure, took over from the Channel Islander, Wace, the task of composing a vernacular dynastic history of the Norman dukes. But after 1173 no one continued John of Marmoutier's work and both Wace and Benoît stopped writing in the 1170s. Robert of Torigni, the abbot of Mont St Michel who acted as godparent at the baptism of Henry II's daughter Eleanor, continued the flourishing Norman tradition of Latin historiography, but after his death in 1186 he had no successor. In England, by contrast, the writing of history took off again after what had been a quiet period mid-century and, in the purely quantitative terms of number of historians at work simultaneously, it flourished in the 1180s and 1190s as never before. Partly encouraged by Richard I's newsletters, English authors such as Howden, Diceto and Newburgh were aware of, and interested in, events in the sterling zone across the Channel and even as far south as Toulouse and the Limousin, but these three were all dead by 1202, and they had no successors with a perspective capable of embracing the whole of what was left of the Angevin Empire after its heartlands had been torn out in 1202–4.

Naturally histories which contained rather more fiction also offered more scope for flexible cultural legitimization of the new political order. Geoffrey of Monmouth's great creation, the figure of

1 J. Dunbabin, *France in the Making 843–1180* (Oxford, 1985), p. 249.

a King Arthur who was not just ruler of Britain but also conqueror of Gaul and Ireland, offered the Angevins a potential imperial mythology which, once they had appropriated it from the Welsh and the Bretons, might match the Charlemagne of the Capetians. Both Henry II and Richard I seem to have been aware of the potential. Henry was associated with the 'discovery' of the bones of Arthur and Guinevere at Glastonbury, and when Richard went on crusade he took an Excalibur with him. But the collapse of 1202–4 meant that the subsequent political resonance of King Arthur was restricted to that of an English king intensifying his rule over the rest of Britain. In any case as the romances of Chrétien of Troyes make plain, the literary magic of Merlin and King Arthur, of the Knights of the Round Table, of Lancelot, Gawain, Perceval and the others, was so great that it had already overflowed the boundaries of the Angevin Empire and become part of the common currency of western European literature.

So it was with virtually every other aspect of Plantagenet culture. There was no such thing as a Plantagenet civilization which both embraced all the people living in the various Angevin dominions and at the same time set them apart from their neighbours. According to Robert of Torigni, Henry built or renovated castles and royal palaces in Normandy, England, Aquitaine, Anjou, Maine and Touraine, i.e. in all the parts of the Angevin Empire. Yet despite the reach of this royal patron there was no distinctively Angevin or Plantagenet style in art and architecture (except perhaps in kitchen design).[2] Nor was there a distinctively Angevin literature. In this context the existence of several different vernaculars, French, English and Occitan – quite apart from the Celtic languages of the north-western periphery – is of little significance. Many political units of the time contained several linguistic communities within their boundaries. In the case of the Angevin Empire French provided an elite *lingua franca* (as did Latin for the clerical elite). Those who belonged to this Plantagenet elite all shared the same condescending view of the 'barbarous' Irish, Scots and Welsh. But so too did the secular and clerical elites of north-western non-Celtic Europe who lived outside the lands ruled over by Henry II and Richard. In London, Rouen, Angers and Poitiers the political, social and religious leaders belonged to essentially the same French-speaking

---

2 Both for the general point and for examples of circular or octagonal kitchen buildings of the Fontevraud type in England and Normandy as well as elsewhere in the Loire valley region see L. Grant, 'Le patronage architectural d'Henri II et de son entourage', *CCM* 37 (1994).

cultural world as their neighbours and rivals in Arras, Paris and Troyes. Further south, in the Midi of the troubadours, they belonged to essentially the same cultural world as their neighbours and rivals in Toulouse, Marseilles and Barcelona.

## DYNASTIC STRUCTURE

Thoughout its term of existence what gave the Angevin Empire its unity was primarily the ruling dynasty. In consequence it was, in the opinion of most historians, unlikely to survive for long. For one thing, when the family quarrelled amongst themselves, the empire itself was put at risk. Even if the head of the firm managed to keep control during his lifetime what would happen when he died? In the débâcle of 1202–4 the quarrel between John and Arthur – uncle and nephew – was to play a major role. For another, both Henry II and Richard as heads of the family had anticipated partitions after their deaths. Had it not been for the deaths of two young men in their twenties, the Young King and Geoffrey of Brittany, the inheritance of 1189 would have looked very different. The custom of partible inheritance was bound to lead to political fragmentation.

In various respects this blindingly obvious generalization is one which has to be qualified. In the first place partition did not necessarily lead to the immediate dismemberment of the empire. Much could depend on the precise terms of the family settlement. Did they include the reservation of an overriding superiority in the hands of the eldest son? Would, in other words, the familial structure of Henry II's day be retained in subsequent generations? It looks as though this is what Henry himself intended. In 1173 and again in 1183 he went to some lengths to obtain from Richard, as duke of Aquitaine, a formal recognition that he owed allegiance (expressed through an act of homage) to his elder brother Henry. It is, of course, true that arrangements which subordinated one brother to another were fraught with tension; in the history of Henry II's family the dates 1173 and 1183 have an ominous ring. Moreover, given what we know of the Young King's character, it seems unlikely that he would have made an effective chairman of the family firm. As it happened, it was Richard, not Henry who succeeded their father and he did retain some overriding authority. Thus his response to John's rebellion in 1193–94 was to confiscate Ireland. But Ireland – restored to John by 1196 – was a relatively simple case, at any rate in legal terms. The legal position on the Continent was complicated by the fact that here the Angevins were the acknowledged subjects of the king of France. For example, Richard's claim to lordship over Brittany and thus to custody of his nephew Arthur, the heir to the duchy, could be, and in 1196 was, countered by Philip Augustus's insistence that as king of France these rights more properly belonged to him. In ways such as this Capetian overlordship tended to weaken the authority of the head of the Angevin family but, even without this additional problem, it is unlikely that that authority could have survived for long. Where the crucial relationship was between father and sons, the notion of seniority might act as a political cement, but between brother and brother it was as much a hindrance as a help. Partition was bound, in the long run, to end in the break-up of the Angevin Empire.

In these circumstances it becomes important to try to assess the likely frequency of partitions. On the one hand, fathers readily contemplated division in order to provide for their sons born or unborn; on the other hand, brothers tended to exclude younger brothers in order to grab everything for themselves. Thus in 1155–56 Henry II refused to carry out the terms of his father's will. When, after the death of the Young King in 1183, Richard became his father's chief heir, he refused to give up Aquitaine in order to make room for John. In 1189 Richard's alliance with Philip Augustus meant that his position was unchallengeable. John remained lord of Ireland; in time Brittany would belong to Geoffrey's posthumous son Arthur (at this date two years old); the rest Richard kept for himself. John, in turn, was unwilling, when his mother died in 1204, to concede Gascony to his brother-in-law Alfonso VIII of Castile. This unaccommodating attitude, combined with the accidents of birth and death, meant that out of the various partition schemes envisaged in 1151 and after, only two actually came into effect: the allocation of Brittany to Geoffrey and his heirs and the allocation of Ireland to John. In other words the unity of the Angevin Empire was, as it happened, very largely preserved – particularly after the accession of John, as Richard's heir, in 1199.

None the less, it might be argued that this was purely accidental and that, so long as fathers wanted to provide for sons, there was one day bound to be a thorough-going partition of the Angevin Empire. The flaw in this argument lies in the fact that although paternal attitudes might well have remained constant, the family estate did not. Family law made a distinction between inheritance and acquisition. What a man inherited he should pass on to his eldest son; what he acquired – whether by conquest, purchase or by marriage – he could dispose of much more freely, often to provide for younger sons. If a man had a single heir, then that heir would receive both inheritance and acquisition and in turn ought to pass both on, now united, to his own eldest son. The father's acquisition would have become the son's patrimony:

> Thus Normandy and England, separable as inheritance and acquisition in 1087, became a single patrimony after 1135; England/Normandy and Maine/Anjou separable under Geoffrey of Anjou, became a single inheritance under Henry II. The Norman/Angevin dominions and the lands of Eleanor of Aquitaine, separable under Henry II, were treated as a single inheritance after 1189.[3]

The Angevin Empire, once a distinctly partible empire, had become, by John's reign, a much more impartible one.

What would have happened if John had managed to keep control of all his dominions? What provision would have been made for his second son, later known as Richard of Cornwall? We shall never know the answers to these questions but it is worth noting that *c.* 1209 Gerald de Barri suggested that Ireland would make a suitable kingdom for a younger son. It looks as though Gerald assumed that all the rest of the Angevin dominions (and claims to dominion) comprised a single inheritance. With Henry III's apanage grant to Edward, his eldest son, in 1254 we are on firmer ground. Edward was given Ireland, Gascony, Oléron and the Channel Islands, as well as estates in England and Wales, but all 'in such manner that the said lands . . . may never be separated from the crown . . . but they should remain to the king of England for ever'. Edward's subordinate role was emphasized by the fact that while his father lived he was never called duke of Aquitaine or lord of Ireland; these titles remained the exclusive prerogative of the king. Clearly, by this time, there was a unified Plantagenet empire – but it can hardly be called an 'Angevin' Empire – since by this date most of the continental lands, including Anjou itself, had been lost. What this development does show, however, is that although the familial structure of the Angevin Empire might have led to its dismemberment, it was not inevitable that it would do so and indeed, as things turned out,

3 J. C. Holt, 'Politics and property in early Medieval England', *Past and Present*, 57 (1972), p. 18.

it did not. On the other hand if the kings of England had retained control of the lands of the dukes of Normandy and counts of Anjou, it might not have been so easy to treat the whole as a single indivisible unit. In these circumstances the kings of France would always have used their position as overlords of the Angevin lands in France to press for a partition, and doubtless, at some time or other, there would have been members of the Angevin dynasty to whom this idea appealed. It was the partibility of the empire, inherent in its structure from the beginning under Henry II, which was virtually certain to be its undoing.

Although by the twelfth century the crown of France, unlike the Angevin Empire, had clearly become indivisible, this did not guarantee that its possessor would enjoy real power throughout the kingdom – far from it. So far as real power was concerned, in the Capetian kingdom, as in the Angevin Empire, much depended upon genealogical accident. When Louis VIII died in 1226 his second, third and fourth sons were granted massive apanages: Artois to the second-born, Anjou and Maine to the third, Poitou and the Auvergne to the fourth. Of his own and his father's territorial gains only Normandy was retained under direct crown control – underlining yet again the priority given to the acquisition and retention of Normandy in Capetian strategic thinking. These apanage grants have often been interpreted as threats to the creation of a powerful French kingdom, threats obviated only because their families died out thus allowing the apanages to 'revert' to the crown. When Philip Augustus died, he was survived by only one unquestionably legitimate son – an accident of birth which has done much to lend an air of permanence to his achievement and make him seem all the greater in the eyes of modern historians. If Louis VII had died without a son – as for a long time seemed likely – the crown of France could well have fallen to an Angevin prince, the Young King, husband of Louis' elder daughter Margaret or, if she died, to the husband of the younger daughter Alice whom Henry II kept in his custody for twenty years. Was she, as Robert-Henri Bautier speculated, being saved for the moment when the Old King was free to marry again? If this combination of genealogical accident and political calculation – no more curious than the actual events of the early 1150s – had come to pass, it might, of course, have worked wonders for the real power of the king of France.

In a fine phrase John Le Patourel pointed out that the Angevin Empire was 'not simply a continuation of the Norman Empire, somewhat enlarged after an unfortunate hiccup'.[4] The point was worth making since the allegedly 'over-extended' Angevin Empire has often been compared unfavourably with the 'compact, tightly-integrated and sturdily independent' Anglo-Norman state.[5] The Angevin Empire has been portrayed as though it were the Norman Empire run to fat and, in consequence, not as well equipped to meet the competitive demands of twelfth-century power politics as its leaner and fitter predecessor had been. Such comparisons are, in Dogberry's phrase, 'odorous'. Whatever the optimum size for a twelfth- or thirteenth-century monarchy may have been, it is hard to demonstrate that the Norman Empire was a 'better' size than the Angevin. Nor can it be shown that an empire which included Anjou and Aquitaine was bound to be weaker than the Norman Empire on the grounds that these territories 'lacked Normandy's tradition of independence from France'. It is true that in March 1202 when Philip summoned John to his court in Paris, he countered John's claim that, as duke of Normandy, he was not bound to meet his suzerain lord anywhere but on their borders, by asserting that John was summoned not as duke of Normandy but as duke of Aquitaine. In the circumstances of the appeal of the Lusignans this was an easy answer. But it would be naïve to believe that, if pushed, Philip could not have found another answer which would have served the same need. In 1151, after all, John's father, as duke of Normandy, had done homage in Paris. And as recently as 1201 John had treated with Philip in Paris. Even if Philip had summoned John to meet him on the frontier, and John had come, Philip could certainly have made demands which John would have refused. For example, pending the sentence of the court, he could have insisted that John hand over vital castles as security. When John refused to hand them over he would be condemned and the confiscation of all the lands he held of the king of France proclaimed. In 1202 indeed Philip actually did demand castles as security – and they were Norman castles, not Aquitanian ones. The point is that Philip was deliberately pushing John into a corner. Somehow or other a legal justification for war was going to be found.

The legal shadow boxing in the political circumstances of 1202

---

4 J. Le Patourel, 'The Norman Conquest, 1066, 1106, 1154', in R. A. Brown (ed.), *Proceedings of the Battle Conference on AngloNorman Studies*, 1978 (Woodbridge, 1979), p. 114.

5 C. W. Hollister, 'Normandy, France and the AngloNorman *Regnum*', *Speculum*, 51 (1976).

tells us very little indeed about genuine differences in status between Normandy and Aquitaine. In reality, geography alone ensured that, except for the years when Louis VII was also duke of Aquitaine, there was at least as much independence in Anjou and Aquitaine as in Normandy. In Anjou there was a tradition which was distinctly hostile to the Capetians, writing them off as usurpers and pseudo-kings. In the papal schism of 1130 when the king of France decided in favour of Innocent II – and was followed by the supposedly independent-minded Henry I – Duke William X of Aquitaine declared for Anacletus II. In 1126, when Henry I sent troops to help Louis VI in the Auvergne, Suger of St-Denis, writing in 1144, described the force as *tributarius de Normannia exercitus*. Henry I might have disliked this formulation but the 1133 inquest into the knight service of Bayeux shows that the view taken at the French court had some basis in Norman custom. According to the returns to the inquest the bishop of Bayeux owed 20 knights to the duke and ten knights, through the duke, to the king of France. No Angevin duke of Normandy ever sent a 'tributary army' to join the host of his Capetian overlord. The standing and power of Henry II and Richard I as dukes of Normandy and kings of England were enhanced not weakened by their possession of Anjou and Aquitaine.

To historians it has very often seemed as though the Capetians were gradually intensifying and increasing their suzerainty over the Angevins. The process began in 1151 when Henry did homage to Louis VII not on the border between their territories (*homage en marche*) but in Paris. Equals meet halfway; subordinates have to attend their lord's court. On the other hand, according to Wace, William I (the hero of the *Roman de Rou*) went to Paris to do homage in 1035. We cannot use Wace's story as evidence for what actually happened in 1035, only as evidence for what one learned Norman thought would be acceptable at Henry II's court in the 1160s and 1170s. And since William I is very much the hero of the *Roman de Rou*, the great conqueror in whose footsteps the present king is following, we can hardly conclude that performing homage in Paris was felt to demean the Norman duke, not at any rate when that duke was Henry II.

In 1200 Philip was promised a 20,000 mark relief in return for recognizing John as Richard's heir. Law tended to be more formally stated in the later twelfth century than it had been fifty or a hundred years earlier. But in practice Norman rebels against Henry I had found it just as easy to appeal to the French king for help as did the

Lusignans in 1201–2. At all times succession disputes and family rivalries created opportunities for the Capetian overlord. It was in such circumstances as these that Philip I of France had made inroads into the Vexin in the 1070s and 1080s. Especially for those who lived close to or across the Norman-Capetian frontier 'the nature of the political game in northern France barely changed in its fundamentals between 1000 and 1200'.[6] What was decisive was not Capetian suzerainty but other matters: the personal qualities of the kings, and the resources available to them.

The legal relationship between a king of France and a king of England who held territories on the Continent meant that it was relatively easy for the king of France to legitimize his own actions as part of a legal process. In this sense, legally speaking, the king of France always had the upper hand and it was bound to be the case that, one day, an able and aggressive king of France would find himself opposed by an inadequate opponent. To this extent the feudal dependence was a structural weakness: the 'fatal weakness' in Le Patourel's view.[7] In the event it proved to be fatal when one of the ablest and most ruthless kings ever to rule France happened to be opposed by one of the worst kings ever to rule England. The kings of France, of course, were singularly fortunate in avoiding succession disputes and family rivalries – until, that is, the outbreak of the Hundred Years' War. Then it would be a different story.

6 D. Bates, 'The rise and fall of Normandy *c.* 911–1204', in D. Bates and A. Curry (eds.), *England and Normandy in the Middle Ages* (London, 1994), p. 24.
7 Le Patourel, 'The Norman Conquest', p. 118.

# Further reading

## ABBREVIATIONS

| | |
|---|---|
| *ANS* | *Anglo-Norman Studies* |
| *CCM* | *Cahiers de Civilisation Médiévale* |
| Church, *King John* | ed. S. D. Church, *King John: New Interpretations* (Woodbridge, 1999) |
| *HSJ* | *Haskins Society Journal* |
| *La cour Plantagenêt* | ed. M. Aurell, *La cour Plantagenêt (1154–1204).* Civilisation Médiévale VIII (Poitiers, 2000) |

In the belief that English-speaking students are already relatively well supplied with bibliographical guides to English history, here I have aimed at providing rather more comprehensive coverage of work in English relating to the Angevin dominions outside England.

## GENERAL PROBLEMS

J. Le Patourel, 'The Plantagenet Dominions', *History,* 50 (1965) remains the most influential brief introduction. See also some of his other essays, notably 'Feudal Empires: Norman and Plantagenet', 'The Norman Conquest, 1066, 1106, 1154?', 'Angevin Successions and the Angevin Empire' all reprinted in his *Feudal Empires: Norman and Plantagenet* (London, 1984).

J. C. Holt, 'The End of the Anglo-Norman Realm', *Proceedings of the British Academy,* 61 (1975), reprinted in his *Magna Carta and Medieval Government* (London, 1985) contains an important discussion of the structure of the Angevin Empire. So also do F. M. Powicke, *The Loss of Normandy* (2nd edn, Manchester, 1960); R. V. Turner 'The Problem of Survival for the Angevin "Empire"', *American Historical Review* 100 (1995); and R. Benjamin, 'The Angevin Empire', *History Today* 36 (February 1986), reprinted in N. Saul (ed.), *England in Europe 1066–1453* (London, 1994). For an eloquent view of the differences between the Norman and Angevin Empires see C. W. Hollister, 'Normandy, France and the Anglo-Norman *Regnum*', *Speculum,* 51 (1976). There are some wide-ranging reflections in R. W. Southern, 'England's First Entry into Europe', in his *Medieval Humanism and Other Studies* (Oxford, 1970).

The papers given at a confererence at Fontevraud, published in *Cahiers de Civilisation Médiévale* 29 (1986), took a thoroughly sceptical view of the coherence of the Plantagenet lands, in particular the summing-up by R. H. Bautier, ' "Empire Plantagenêt" ou "Espace Plantagenêt". Y-a-t-il eu une civilisation du monde Plantagenêt?' On the problems of succession see J. C. Holt's paper at the same conference, 'Aliénor d'Aquitaine, Jean sans Terre et la succession de 1199'; also his 'The Casus Regis: The Law and Politics of Succession in the Plantagenet Dominions, 1185–1247', in J. C. Holt, *Colonial England 1066–1215* (London, 1997). For the legal position at the end of the empire see J. R. Studd, 'The Lord Edward and Henry III', *Bulletin of the Institute of Historical Research*, 50 (1977); for the importance of the memory of the Angevin Empire, M. Vale, *The Angevin Legacy and the Hundred Years War 1250–1340* (Oxford, 1990).

K. Norgate, *England under the Angevin Kings* (2 vols, London, 1887) still retains its value as a fine narrative (up to 1206); despite its title, it covers much more than England. The most comprehensive modern study, also wider in scope than its title suggests, is J. Boussard, *Le gouvernement d'Henri II Plantagenêt* (Paris, 1956). Its 90 pages of index make it an invaluable work of reference.

## FRANCE

Helpful guides in English to the political scene in France are: J. Dunbabin, *France in the Making, 843–1180* (Oxford, 1985), including a good concise discussion of the Angevin Empire; E. M. Hallam, *Capetian France, 987–1328* (London, 1980); K. F. Werner, 'Kingdom and Principalities in Twelfth-Century France', in T. Reuter (ed. and trans.), *The Medieval Nobility* (Amsterdam, 1979); R. Fawtier, *The Capetian Kings of France* (London, 1960).

## FRENCH LOCAL AND REGIONAL STUDIES

On the border lands of the Angevin Empire see: D. Power, 'What did the Frontier of Angevin Normandy Comprise?', *ANS* 17 (1994); D. Power, 'French and Norman Frontiers in the Central Middle Ages'. in D. Power and N. Standen (eds.), *Frontiers in Question: Eurasian Borderlands 700–1700* (London, 1999); J. Green, 'Lords of the Norman Vexin', in J. Gillingham and J. C. Holt (eds.), *War and Government in the Middle Ages* (Woodbridge, 1984); D. Power 'Between the Angevin and Capetian Courts: John de Rouvray and the Knights of the Pays de Bray, 1180–1225', in K. S. B. Keats-Rohan (ed.), *Family Trees and the Roots of Politics* (Woodbridge, 1997). K. Thompson, 'The Lords of Laigle: Ambition and Insecurity on the

Borders of Normandy', *ANS* 18 (1995); K. Thompson, *Power and Border Lordship: The County of the Perche 1000–1226* (forthcoming). For a 'border province', see G. Devailly, *Le Berry du Xe siècle jusqu'au milieu du XIIIe siècle* (Paris, 1973). On the greatest of frontier castles see D. Pitte, *Château-Gaillard* (Vernon, France, 1996).

## Normandy

On Normandy after 1142 (the death of Orderic Vitalis) there is as yet little to compare with the rich literature on the time of William the Conqueror and his sons, but see C. H. Haskins, *Norman Institutions* (New York, 1918); L. Musset, *Huit essais sur l'autorité ducale en Normandie (Xie–XIIe siècles)*, Cahier no. 17, *Annales de Normandie*, 1985; D. Bates, 'The Rise and Fall of Normandy *c.* 911–1204', in D. Bates and A. Curry (eds.), *England and Normandy in the Middle Ages* (London, 1994); D. Bates, 'Rouen 900 to 1204: From Scandinavian Settlement to Angevin "Capital" ', in J. Stratford (ed.), *Medieval Art, Architecture and Archaeology at Rouen*, British Archaeological Association, Conference Transactions 12 (1993); M. Billoré, 'La noblesse normande dans l'entourage de Richard Ier', in *La cour Plantagenêt*. D. Crouch, *The Beaumont Twins: The Roots and Branches of Power in the Twelfth Century* (Cambridge, 1986) deals with this most powerful Anglo-Norman family from 1120 to 1168.

## Brittany

J. A. Everard, *Brittany and the Angevins: Province and Empire 1158–1203* (Cambridge, 2000); J. Everard and M. Jones (eds.), *The Charters of Duchess Constance of Brittany and her Family, 1171–1221* (Woodbridge, 1999). B. A. Pocquet du Haut-Jussé, 'Les Plantagenêts et la Bretagne', *Annales de Bretagne*, 53 (1946); Y. Hillion, 'La Bretagne et la rivalité Capétiens-Plantagenêts: Un exemple – la duchesse Constance, 1186–1202', *Annales de Bretagne*, 92 (1985); J. Everard, 'The "Justiciarship" in Brittany and Ireland under Henry II', *ANS* 20 (1997).

## Anjou

J. Boussard, *Le comté d'Anjou sous Henri Plantagenêt et ses fils, 1151–1204* (Paris, 1938). On the great castle of Chinon, see S. Rocheteau, 'Le château de chinon aux XIIe et XIII siècles', in *La cour Plantagenét*.

## Poitou

A. Richard, *Histoire des comtes de Poitou, 778–1204* (2 vols, Paris, 1903); A. Debord, A., *La Société laïque dans les Pays de la Charente X–XII siècles*

(Paris, 1984); G. T. Beech, *A Rural Society in Medieval France: The Gatine of Poitou in the Eleventh and Twelfth Centuries* (Baltimore, 1964); R. Hajdu, 'Castles, Castellans and the Structure of Politics in Poitou, 1152–1271', *Journal of Medieval History,* 4 (1978). It is instructive to compare this with the English evidence set out by R. A. Brown, 'A List of Castles, 1154–1216', *English Historical Review* (1959). S. Painter, 'The Lords of Lusignan in the Eleventh and Twelfth Centuries', *Speculum* 32 (1957), 'Castellans of the Plain of Poitou in the Eleventh and Twelfth Centuries', *Speculum* 31 (1956) and 'The Houses of Lusignan and Châtellerault, 1150–1250', *Speculum* 30 (1955), all reprinted in his *Feudalism and Liberty* (Baltimore, 1961). For two recent architectural studies, see M-P. Baudry, 'Les châteaux des Lusignans en Poiton: 1152–1242', in *Isabelle d'Angoulême comtesse-reine et son temps,* Civilisation Médiévale V (Poitiers, 1999) and M-P. Baudry, 'Les fortifications des Plantagenêts à Thouars', in *La cour Plantagenêt*. N. Vincent, 'The Poitevins in the Household of Henry II', in *La cour Plantagenêt* is a fundamental study of Henry II's personal involvement – or lack of it – in the government of Poitou.

## Gascony

C. Higounet, *Bordeaux pendant le haut moyen âge* (Bordeaux, 1963); Y. Renouard, *Bordeaux sous les rois d'Angleterre* (Bordeaux, 1965); F. B. Marsh, *English Rule in Gascony, 1199–1259* (Ann Arbor, MI, 1912); P. Tucoo-Chala, *La vicomté de Béarn et le problème de sa souveraineté* (Bordeaux, 1961).

## ANGEVIN TRADING ZONE

Indications of the commercial importance of western France are to be found in C. Petit-Dutaillis, *The French Communes in the Middle Ages* (Amsterdam, 1979); some of the essays in Y. Renouard, *Etudes d'histoire médiévale* (2 vols, Paris, 1968); R. Dion, *Histoire de la vigne et du vin en France des origines au XIXe siècle* (Paris, 1959); and P. Boissonade, 'La renaissance et l'essor de la vie et du commerce maritimes en Poitou, Aunis et Saintonge', *Revue d'histoire économique et sociale,* 12 (1924). B. T. Hudson, 'The Changing Economy of the Irish Sea Province', in B. Smith, *Britain and Ireland, 900–1300* (Cambridge, 1999) puts this zone in British and Irish perspective; see also A. O'Brien, 'Commercial Relations between Aquitaine and Ireland *c.* 1000 to *c.* 1500', in J. M. Picard (ed.), *Aquitaine and Ireland in the Middle Ages* (Dublin, 1995).

On mints and the circulation of coinage, see F. Dumas, 'La monnaie dans les domaines Plantagenêt', *CCM* 29 (1986). F. Dumas, 'La monnaie dans le royaume au temps de Philippe Auguste', in R. H. Bautier (ed.), *La France de Philippe Auguste: Le temps de mutations* (Paris, 1982) and J. Yvon, 'Esterlins à la croix courte dans les trésors français de la fin du XII$^e$ et de la première moitié du XIII$^e$ siècle', *British Numismatic Journal*, 39 (1970).

## ENGLAND

Good general surveys include R. Mortimer, *Angevin England 1154–1258* (Oxford, 1994); M. T. Clanchy, *England and its Rulers, 1066–1272* (2nd edn, London, 1998); F. Barlow, *The Feudal Kingdom of England, 1042–1216* (5th edn, London, 1999); R. Bartlett, *England under the Norman and Angevin Kings 1075–1225* (Oxford, 2000).

## BRITAIN AND IRELAND

For excellent introductions to the Angevin orbit in Britain see R. Frame, *The Political Development of the British Isles* (Oxford, 1990), R. R. Davies, *The First English Empire* (Oxford, 2000) and R. R. Davies, *Domination and Conquest: The Experience of Ireland, Scotland and Wales, 1100–1300* (Cambridge, 1990). Despite its title D. Walker, *The Normans in Britain* (Oxford, 1995) takes the story up to the early thirteenth century. On perceptions of the 'Celtic Fringe', see Chapters 6 and 7 in R. Bartlett, *Gerald of Wales* (Oxford, 1982) and some of the essays in J. Gillingham, *The English in the Twelfth Century* (Woodbridge, 2000) – 'The Beginnings of English Imperialism'; 'The English Invasion of Ireland'; 'Conquering the Barbarians: War and Chivalry in Britain and Ireland'; and 'The Foundations of a Disunited Kingdom'.

### Wales

R. R. Davies, *Conquest, Coexistence and Change: Wales, 1063–1415* (Oxford, 1987); A. D. Carr, *Medieval Wales* (London, 1995); R. R. Davies, 'Kings, Lords and Liberties in the March of Wales', *Transactions of the Royal Historical Society*, 5th series, 29 (1979); 'Henry II, Richard I and the Lord Rhys', in J. Gillingham, *The English in the Twelfth Century* (Woodbridge, 2000); I. W. Rowlands, 'King John and Wales', in Church, *King John*.

### Ireland

*A New History of Ireland, ii, Medieval Ireland, 1169–1534*, ed. A. Cosgrove (Oxford, 1987) has been well described as 'a gigantic lucky dip' by R. Frame, whose own *Colonial Ireland 11691–1369* (Dublin, 1972) offers a good brief sketch. So also does S. Duffy, *Ireland in the Middle Ages* (Dublin, 1997). A. J. Otway-Ruthven, A *History of Medieval Ireland* (2nd edn, London, 1980). Fundamental to the study of the Angevin intrusion into Ireland is M. T. Flanagan, *Irish Society, Anglo-Norman Settlers, Angevin Kingship* (Oxford, 1989). See also M. T. Flanagan, 'Strongbow, Henry II and Anglo-Norman Intervention in Ireland', in J. Gillingham and J. C. Holt (eds), *War and Government in the Middle Ages* (Woodbridge, 1984) and B. Smith, *Colonisation and Conquest in Medieval Ireland: The English in Louth, 1170–1330* (Cambridge, 1999). On Angevin government in Ireland, see M. T. Flanagan, 'Household Favourites: Angevin Royal Agents in Ireland under Henry II and John', in *Seanchas, Studies in Honour of F. J. Byrne*, ed. A. P. Smyth (Dublin, 2000). There are useful essays by S. Duffy, 'The First Ulster Plantation: John de Courcy and the Men of Cumbria', by B. Smith, 'Tenure and Locality in North Leinster in the Early Thirteenth Century', and by H. Perros, 'Crossing the Shannon Frontier: Connacht and the Anglo-Normans, 1170–1224', in T. Barry, R. Frame and K. Simms (eds), *Colony and Frontier in Medieval Ireland* (London, 1995). S. Duffy, 'John and Ireland: The Origins of England's Irish Problem', in Church, *King John* disposes of the notion that John had a well-considered view of politics and government of Ireland.

## Scotland

A. A. M. Duncan, *Scotland: The Making of the Kingdom* (Edinburgh, 1975). G. W. S. Barrow, *Kingship and Unity: Scotland, 1000–1306* (London, 1981); K. J. Stringer, *Earl David of Huntingdon. A Study in Anglo-Scottish History* (Edinburgh, 1985); D. D. R. Owen, *William the Lion: Kingship and Culture 1143–1214* (East Linton, 1997); A. A. M. Duncan, 'John King of England and the Kings of Scots', in Church, *King John.*

## RELATIONS WITH OTHER POWERS

The section on the Angevin Empire in G. P. Cuttino, *English Medieval Diplomacy* (Bloomington, 1985) is thin. But J. Ahlers, *Die Welfen und die englischen Könige 1165–1235* (Hildesheim, 1987) provides an exceptionally useful survey. See also N. Fryde, 'King John and the Empire' in Church, *King John.* Also J. P. Huffman, *The Social Politics of Medieval Diplomacy: Anglo-German Relations 1066–1307* (Michigan, 2000). On relations with Toulouse, R. Benjamin, 'A Forty Years War: Toulouse and the Plantagenets, 1156–96', *Historical Research* 61 (1988).

## RULERS

In a field where much depended on personal and family relationships, studies of the individual Angevin rulers, beginning with M. Chibnall, *The Empress Matilda* (Oxford, 1991) remain important.

### Henry II

W. L. Warren, *Henry II* (London, 1973) is both massive and readable and remains indispensable, though its perspective is Anglo-British rather than French. There are two useful studies of the beginnings of the reign, E. Amt, *The Accession of Henry II in England: Royal Government Restored, 1149–1159* (Woodbridge, 1993) and G. J. White, *Restoration and Reform, 1153–1165: Recovery from Civil War in England* (Cambridge, 2000). Most work on Henry II has focused on his involvement with English law and government; for comment see my 'Conquering Kings: Some Twelfth-Century Reflections on Henry II and Richard I', in J. Gillingham, *Richard Coeur de Lion* (London, 1994).

### Richard I

K. Norgate, *Richard the Lionheart* (London, 1924), like all her work, has worn well. The best succinct sketch is to be found in J. O. Prestwich, 'Richard Coeur de Lion: *Rex Bellicosus*', in J. L. Nelson (ed.), *Richard Coeur de Lion in History and Myth* (London, 1992). See also U. Kessler, *Richard I. Löwenherz: König, Kreuzritter, Abenteurer* (Graz, 1995) and, most recently, J. Gillingham, *Richard I* (New Haven and London, 1999) and J. Flori, *Richard Coeur de Lion. Le roi-chevalier* (Paris, 1999). The latter is particularly valuable for its exposition of the chivalrous milieu. Two articles by R. Heiser, 'The Sheriffs of Richard I: Trends of Management as Seen in the Shrieval Appointments from 1189 to 1194', *HSJ* 4 (1992) and 'Richard I and His Appointments to English Shrievalties', *English Historical Review* 112 (1997) have drawn attention to the king's managerial skills.

### John

The indispensable guide to recent work is S. Church (ed.), *King John: New Interpretations* (Woodbridge, 1999). This includes important reassessments of the economic climate in England, the 'inflation question', by J. L. Bolton, 'The English Economy in the Early Thirteenth Century', and P. Latimer, 'Early Thirteenth-Century Prices'. S. Painter, *The Reign of King John* (Baltimore, 1949); W. L. Warren, *King John* (London, 1961); J. C. Holt, *King John* (Historical Association, London, 1963); R. V. Turner, *King John* (London, 1994).

## Henry III

On the early years of his reign there are now two excellent studies, R. Stacey, *Politics, Policy and Finance under Henry III 1216–1245* (Oxford, 1987); and D. A. Carpenter's detailed analytical narrative, *The Minority of Henry III* (London, 1990).

## Capetians

M. Pacaut, *Louis VII et son royaume* (Paris, 1964); C. Petit-Dutaillis, *Etude sur la vie et le règne de Louis VIII* (Paris, 1894) and J. Richard, *Saint Louis* (Paris, 1983).

The most thorough narrative of the reign of Philip Augustus remains A. Cartellieri, *Philipp II: König von Frankreich*, 4 vols, (Leipzig, 1899–1922), but in J. Bradbury, *Philip Augustus, King of France 1180–1223* (London, 1998) there is at last a helpful general account of the Angevins' greatest enemy readily accessible to English readers. The title of J. W. Baldwin's admirable study, *The Government of Philip Augustus* (Berkeley, 1986) is self-explanatory. See also C. W. Hollister and J. W. Baldwin, 'The Rise of Administrative Kingship', *American Historical Review*, 83 (1978). Aspects of his reign are dealt with by G. Duby, *Le dimanche de Bouvines* (Paris, 1973) and in the collection of essays ed. R. H. Bautier, *La France de Philippe Auguste: le temps de mutations* (Paris, 1982).

## Queens

J. Martindale, 'Eleanor of Aquitaine', in J. L. Nelson (ed.), *Richard Coeur de Lion in History and Myth* (London, 1992), reprinted in J. Martindale, *Status, Authority and Regional Power. Aquitaine and France 9th to 12th centuries* (Aldershot, 1997); J. Martindale, 'Eleanor of Aquitaine: The Last Years', in Church, *King John*; W. W. Kibler (ed.), *Eleanor of Aquitaine: Patron and Politician* (Austin, TX, 1977); M. Hivergneaux, 'Aliénor d'Aquitaine: le pouvoir d'une femme à la lumière de ses chartes (1152–1204)', in *La cour Plantagenêt*; A. Trindade, *Berengaria: In Search of Richard the Lionheart's Queen* (Dublin, 1999); N. Vincent, 'Isabella of Angoulême: John's Jezebel', in Church, *King John*.

## OTHER BIOGRAPHIES

Helpful studies of individuals active in Angevin politics include: S. Painter, *William Marshal* (Baltimore, 1933), C. R. Cheney, *Hubert Walter* (London, 1967). C. R. Young, *Hubert Walter: Lord of Canterbury and Lord of England* (Durham, N. Carolina, 1967). J. W. Alexander, *Ranulf of Chester*

(Athens, Georgia, 1983). D. Crouch, *William Marshal: Court, Career and Chivalry in the Angevin Empire* (London, 1990). C. P. Schriber, *The Dilemma of Arnulf of Lisieux* (Bloomington, 1990). N. Vincent, *Peter des Roches: An Alien in English Politics 1205–1238* (Cambridge, 1996). In his *Men Raised from the Dust: Administrative Service and Upward Mobility in Angevin England* (Philadelphia, 1988) R. V. Turner offers six mini-biographies. For an ecclesiastic, failed politician and successful author who took a generally jaundiced view of the Angevin kings see the superb intellectual biography, R. Bartlett, *Gerald of Wales* (1982). L. Grant, *Abbot Suger of St Denis* (London, 1998), takes a forthright view of the churchman/politician who was a key figure at the Capetian court during the making of the Angevin Empire.

## MAKING THE EMPIRE

There is no full-length study of the Angevin conquest of Normandy and England, but see the stimulating essay by C. W. Hollister and T. K. Keefe, 'The Making of the Angevin Empire', *Journal of British Studies,* 12 (1973) and Chapter 4, 'The End', in J. Le Patourel, *The Norman Empire* (Oxford, 1976): pp. 322–5 contain some useful observations on the term 'empire'. Most studies of Stephen's reign, for example, R. H. C. Davis, *King Stephen* (3rd edn, London, 1990), have concentrated, as Stephen himself did, on events in England, but the most recent narrative comes from a scholar as much at home in Norman history as in English, D.Crouch, *The Reign of King Stephen* (London, 2000). See also M. Chibnall, 'Normandy', in E. King (ed.), *The Anarchy of King Stephen's Reign* (Oxford, 1994). K. J. Stringer, *The Reign of Stephen* (London, 1993) is very useful concise account. The title of T. K. Keefe, 'Geoffrey Plantagenet's Will and the Angevin Succession', *Albion,* 6 (1974), is selfexplanatory; for a different interpretation, see B. S. Bachrach, 'The Idea of the Angevin Empire', *Albion* 10 (1978).

## GOVERNMENT

Given disparities in the volume of evidence it is natural that work on Angevin government should have concentrated on England, though J. Boussard, 'Les institutions de l'empire plantagenêt', in vol. I of F. Lot and R. Fawtier (eds), *Histoire des institutions françaises au moyen âge* (Paris, 1953) is a notable exception. The best starting-point is probably J. E. A. Jolliffe, *Angevin Kingship* (2nd edn, London, 1963). Jolliffe's chapters on the king's household can now be supplemented by S. D. Church, *The Household Knights of King John* (Cambridge, 1999), and all put in perspective by J. O. Prestwich, 'The Place of the Royal Household in English History, 1066–1307', *Medieval History* 1 (1991).

The records of central government are discussed by H. Jenkinson,

'Financial Records of the Reign of King John', in H. E. Maldon (ed.), *Magna Carta Commemoration Essays* (London, 1917) and by H. G. Richardson in his introduction to *The Memoranda Roll for the Michaelmas Term of the First Year of the Reign of King John* (London, 1943). The procedures and traditions of the English exchequer in the 1170s are vividly set out in Richard FitzNigel's remarkable treatise, 'The Dialogue of the Exchequer', in C. Johnson (ed.), *Dialogus de Scaccario* (London, 1950), but H. G. Richardson and G. O. Sayles, *The Governance of Medieval England* (Edinburgh, 1963), especially chapters 8, 11, 12 and 13, argue forcefully that it was the chamber, not the exchequer, which was central. For a helpful recalculation of English exchequer revenues see N. Barratt, 'The Revenues of King John', *English Historical Review* 111 (1996) and 'The English Revenues of Richard I' (forthcoming).

An important start has now been made on the badly neglected subject of the Norman exchequer and Norman revenues: V. Moss, 'The Norman Fiscal Revolution 1193–98', in R. Bonney and M. Ormrod (eds.), *Crises, Revolutions and Self-Sustained Fiscal Growth* (Stamford, 1999); V. Moss, 'Normandy and England in 1180: The Pipe Roll Evidence', in D. Bates and A. Curry (eds.), *England and Normandy in the Middle Ages* (London, 1994); V. Moss, 'The Norman Exchequer Rolls of King John', in Church, *King John*.

The all-important relationship between king and provincial government (in this case between Richard I and England) has been analysed by J. C. Holt, 'Ricardus rex Anglorum et dux Normannorum', in his *Magna Carta and Medieval Government* (London, 1985) which can be supplemented by J. T. Appleby's narrative of events in his *England Without Richard, 1189–1199* (London, 1965). See also C. Fagnen, ' Le vocabulaire du pouvoir dans les actes de Richard Cœur de Lion, duc de Normandie', *Actes du Cent Cinquième Congrès national des sociétés savantes, Caen 1980* (Paris, 1984). On the justiciar's role, see F. J. West, *The Justiciarship in England, 1066–1232* (Cambridge, 1966) and D. Bates, 'The Origins of the Justiciarship', *ANS* 4 (1981)

## PATRONAGE

### Secular

The biographies of William Marshal offer the most convenient points of access into the world of court and patronage. For a fascinating insight into the wheeling and dealing involved see N. Vincent, 'William Marshal, King Henry II and the Honour of Châteauroux', *Archives* 25 (2000). Otherwise most work, including the best study of the politics of patronage in this period, J. C. Holt, *The Northerners* (revised edn, Oxford, 1992) has tended to concentrate on England. See also J. E. Lally, 'Secular Patronage at the Court of Henry II', *Bulletin of the Institute of Historical Research*, 49 (1976). T. K. Keefe consciously used English records in quantitative fashion in order to write a qualitative history of patronage; thus his *Feudal Assessments and the Political Community under Henry II and his Sons* (Berkeley, 1983); 'King Henry II and the Earls: The Pipe Roll Evidence', *Albion* 13 (1981); 'Counting Those Who Count: A Computer-Assisted Analysis of Charter Witness-Lists and the Itinerant Court in the First Year of the Reign of King Richard I', *HSJ* 1 (1989) 'Proffers for Heirs and Heiresses in the Pipe Rolls: Some Observations on Indebtedness in the Years before the Magna Carta', *HSJ* 5 (1993).

## *Ecclesiastical*

The wider geographical spread of ecclesiastical records has permitted study of ecclesiastical patronage to move more readily beyond England, e.g. D. Spear, 'The Norman Empire and the Secular Clergy, 1066–1204', *Journal of British Studies*, 21 (1982), D. Spear, 'Power, Patronage and Personality in the Norman Cathedral Chapters, 911–1204', *ANS* 20 (1997). D. Walker, 'Crown and Episcopacy under the Normans and Angevins', *ANS* 5, 1982. O. Pontal, 'Les évêques dans le monde Plantagenêt', *CCM* 29 (1986); R. V. Turner 'Richard Lionheart and English Episcopal Elections', *Albion* 29 (1997); R. V. Turner, 'Richard Lionheart and the Episcopate in his French Domains', *French Historical Studies* 21 (1998); M. Murphy, 'Balancing the Concerns of Church and State: The Archbishops of Dublin, 1181–1228', in T. Barry, R. Frame and K. Simms (eds), *Colony and Frontier in Medieval Ireland* (London, 1995).

## RULERS AND RELIGIOUS

The relationship between ruler and regular clergy has been investigated by E. M. Hallam, 'Henry II, Richard I and the Order of Grandmont', *Journal of Medieval History*, 1 (1975) and 'Henry II as a Founder of Monasteries', *Journal of Ecclesiastical History*, 28 (1977). P.-R. Gaussin, 'Y a-t-il eu une politique monastique des Plantagenêt', *CCM* 29 (1986). For a particularly important case see T. S. R. Boase, 'Fontevraud and the Plantagenets', *Journal of the British Archaeological Association*, 3rd series, 24 (1971), J.-M. Bienvenu, 'Aliénor d'Aquitaine et Fontevraud' *CCM* 29 (1986) and J.-M. Bienvenu, 'Henri II Plantegenêt et Fontevraud' *CCM* 37 (1994). K. Leyser, 'The Angevin Kings and the Holy Man', in, Henry Mayr-Harting (ed.), *Saint Hugh of Lincoln* (Oxford, 1987). E. Mason, 'Rocamadour in Quercy Above All Other Churches: The Healing of Henry II', *Studies in Church History* 19 (1983); E. Bozoky, 'Le culte des saintes et des reliques dans la politique des premiers rois Plantagenêt', in *La cour Plantagenêt.*

## LAW AND CUSTOM

On the place of provincial custom. within the Angevin Empire (as opposed to the vast literature on English Common Law), see J. Yver, 'Les caractères originaux du groupe de coutumes de l'ouest de la France', *Revue historique de droit français et étranger,* 4th series, 30 (1952); J. Yver, 'Le *Très ancien coutumier* de Normandie, miroir de la législation ducale?', *Revue d'histoire du droit,* 39 (1971); P. Hyams, 'The Common Law and the French Connection', *ANS* 4, 1981; P. Brand, 'Ireland and the Literature of the Early Common Law', *Irish Jurist,* new series, 16 (1981), reprinted in P. Brand, *The Making of The Common Law* (London, 1992).

## CRISIS AND FALL

F. M. Powicke, *The Loss of Normandy* (2nd edn, Manchester, 1960), though confusingly arranged, remains fundamental. On the matter of the homage owed to kings of France see K. van Eickels, ' "Homagium" and "Amicitia": Rituals of Peace and their Significance in the Anglo-French Negotiations of the Twelfth Century', *Francia* 24/1 (1997); also S. Reynolds, *Fiefs and Vassals* (Oxford, 1994), pp. 272–6. The view that Philip Augustus was at least as rich as John and that this, at least in part, explains John's defeats in 1203–4, was first put forward by F. Lot and R. Fawtier, *Le premier budget de la monarchie française: le compte général de 1202–1203* (Paris, 1932). It has since been elaborated by J. C. Holt, 'The Loss of Normandy and Royal Finance', in J. Gillingham and J. C. Holt (eds), *War and Government in the Middle Ages* (Woodbridge, 1984). Also tending towards the same conclusion is the argument of J. W. Baldwin, 'La décennie décisive: les années 1190–1203 dans le règne de Philippe Auguste', *Revue Historique,* 266 (1981). But for new calculations relating both to 1202–3 and 1214 see N. Barratt, 'The Revenues of John and Philip Augustus Revisited', in Church, *King John.* It is at any rate clear that in the 1220s the Capetians were much richer than Henry III, see M. Nortier and J. W. Baldwin, 'Contributions à l'étude des finances de Philippe Auguste', *Bibliothèque de l'Ecole des Chartes,* 138 (1980) and D. A. Carpenter, *The Minority of Henry III* (London, 1990). Non-financial matters are stressed by D. Power, 'King John and the Norman Aristocracy', and J. Gillingham, 'Historians without Hindsight: Coggeshall, Diceto and Howden on the Early Years of John's Reign', both in Church, *King John.* For a more critical view of Richard's legacy to John, see R. V. Turner, 'Good or Bad

Kingship? The Case of Richard Lionheart', *HSJ* 8 (1996/1999). For other aspects see E. Audouin, *Essai sur l'armée royale au temps de Philippe Auguste* (Paris, 1913); P. Contamine, 'L'armée de Philippe Auguste' in R-H. Bautier (ed.), *La France de Philippe Auguste: Le temps de mutations* (Paris, 1982); C. Coulson, 'Fortress Policy in Capetian Tradition and Angevin Practice. Aspects of the Conquest of Normandy by Philip II', in *ANS* 6 1983.

## PLANTAGENET CIVILIZATION?

The socio-political content has been well described by M. Aurell, 'La cour Plantagenêt: entourage, savoir at civilité', in *La cour Plantagenêt*. For properly sceptical approaches to questions of direct royal patronage, see K. M. Broadhurst, 'Henry II of England and Eleanor of Aquitaine: Patrons of Literature in French', *Viator* 27 (1996); P. Johanek, 'König Arthur und die Plantagenets' *Frühmittelalterliche Studien*, 21 (1987); P. Bec, 'Troubadours, trouvères et espace Plantagenêt' *CCM* 29 (1986). On Wace and Benoît, J. Blacker, *The Faces of Time: Portrayal of the Past in Old French and Latin Historical Narrative of the Anglo-Norman Regnum* (Austin, TX, 1994), P. Damian-Grint, *The New Historians of the Twelfth-Century Renaissance* (Woodbridge, 1999); and E. Van Houts, 'Wace as Historian', in K. S. B. Keats-Rohan (ed.), *Family Trees and the Roots of Politics* (Woodbridge, 1997). On historians writing in Latin in England see the relevant chapters in A. Gransden's invaluable survey, *Historical Writing in England c.550 to c.1307* (London, 1974), and J. Gillingham, 'Royal Newsletters, Forgeries and English Historians: Some Links between Court and History in the Reign of Richard I' in *La cour Plantagenêt*; in Normandy, L. Shopkow, *History and Community: Norman Historical Writing in the Eleventh and Twelfth Centuries* (Washington, DC, 1997); E. Van Houts, 'Le roi et son historien: Henri II Plantagenêt et Robert de Torigni, abbé du Mont-Saint-Michel', *CCM* 37 (1994).

On the question of a Plantagenet architecture, see above all L. Grant, 'Le patronage architectural d'Henri II et de son entourage', *CCM* 37 (1994); also L. Grant, 'Architectural Relationships between England and Normandy 1100–1204', in D. Bates and A. Curry (eds), *England and Normandy in the Middle Ages* (London, 1994) and A. Mussat, 'L'espace et le temps Plantagenêt: les problèmes d'une architecture', *CCM* 29 (1986) and C. Andrault-Schmitt, 'Le mécénat architectural en question: les chantiers de Saint-Yrieix, Granmont et Le Pin à l'époque de Henri II', in *La cour Plantagenêt*.

# Index